The **Quilter's Bible**

The **Quilter's Bible**

Essential quilting and patchwork
techniques to improve your skills

Edited by Ruth Patrick

CHARTWELL
BOOKS, INC.

A QUARTO BOOK

Published in 2009 by
Chartwell Books, Inc.
A division of Book Sales, Inc.
276 Fifth Avenue, Suite 206
New York, New York 10001
USA

ISBN 13: 978-0-7858-2553-1
ISBN-10: 0-7858-2553-3
QUAR.TQB

Conceived, designed, and produced by
Quarto Publishing plc
The Old Brewery
6 Blundell Street
London N7 9BH

Senior editor: Ruth Patrick
Art editor: Julie Francis
Design assistant: Saffron Stocker
Picture researcher: Sarah Bell
Proofreader: Liz Dalby
Indexer: Ann Barrett

Art director: Caroline Guest
Creative director: Moira Clinch
Publisher: Paul Carslake

Manufactured in Singapore by Pica
  Digital International Pte Ltd.
Printed in China by Midas Printing
  International Ltd.

Contents

Anatomy of the quilt   6

CHAPTER 1
Tools and materials   8

CHAPTER 2
Designing a quilt   20

CHAPTER 3
Basic techniques   42

CHAPTER 4
Blocks   62

CHAPTER 5
Making the top quilt   90

CHAPTER 6
Quilting and finishing   104

CHAPTER 7
Block and quilt directory   122

CHAPTER 8
Resources   182
  Glossary   184
  Useful addresses   187
  Index   188
  Symbols   192
  Acknowledgments   192

Anatomy of the quilt

The craft of quilt-making uses a range of technical terms to distinguish different parts of the quilt. Key aspects of this "anatomy" are illustrated opposite. It is important to remember that the quilt itself is basically a fabric sandwich consisting of three layers: the top (often covered with decorative patchwork or appliqué), the filler, and the backing. The sandwich is held together by the quilting, which is often also an important decorative feature. The binding finishes the edges of the quilt to neaten and enclose the raw edges and filler.

It is worth pointing out the technical distinction between patchwork and appliqué. Patchwork, also known as piecing, is the technique of sewing small pieces of fabric together to create a large piece. Appliqué is the technique of cutting out pieces of fabric and stitching them to a background, usually to create a pictorial or representational design.

A quilt in progress, showing the Morning Star design. A freestanding quilting frame helps to keep the quilt taut over the area that is being worked.

Quilt top (see pages 90–103)
The top layer of the quilt, which can be patchwork, appliqué, or wholecloth.

Sashing or lattice strips (see pages 38–39 and pages 102–103)
A grid of fabric strips that can be used to separate out and to frame the blocks.

Quilting (see page 104–121)
Stitching, often decorative, which holds the three layers of the quilt together.

Batting (see page 18)
The warm interlining or filler forming the inner layer of the quilt.

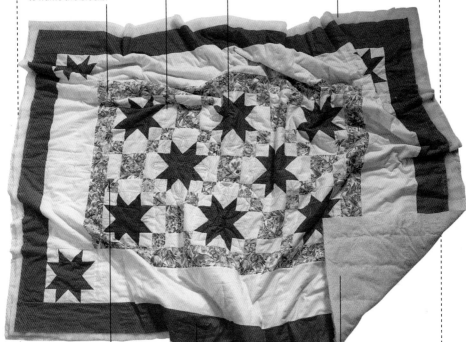

Blocks (see pages 62–89)
The design unit made from either patchwork or appliqué or a combination of the two repeated to make the quilt top. These can be set straight or "on point," that is, diagonally so they form a diamond shape.

Border (see page 40 and pages 102–103)
A frame surrounding the main part of the quilt. It can be plain or patchwork.

Backing (see page 17)
The fabric on the back of the quilt.

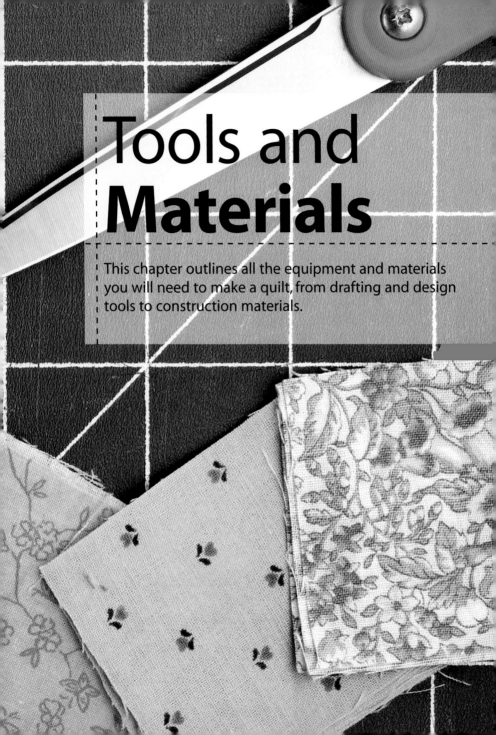

Tools and
Materials

This chapter outlines all the equipment and materials
you will need to make a quilt, from drafting and design
tools to construction materials.

Tools

Everything you need for quilt-making, from drafting and designing to quilting and finishing, is listed on pages 10–15. There are many more aids and tools available from specialist suppliers, but these are the indispensable ones. Of course, one person's useful tool may be another person's useless gadget, so don't be afraid to try out other pieces of equipment just because they're not mentioned here. Aim to buy quality equipment, even if it's a little more expensive. In the long term, you'll find that it's money well spent and you will save a lot of time and frustration.

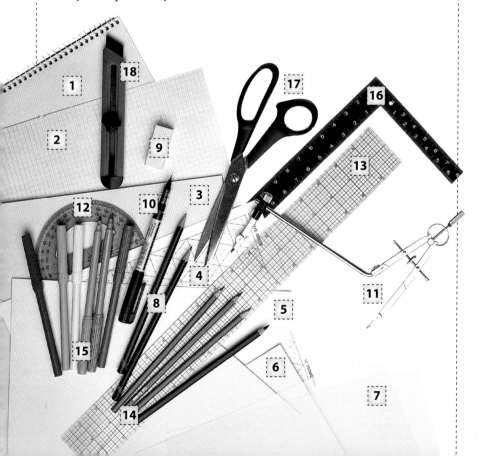

Drafting and design tools

For drafting and design, you will need all the following items, most of which can be obtained from any good arts and crafts retailer. Again, invest in quality and update your supply regularly.

1 Drawing paper for drafting full-size blocks.
2 Graph paper.
3 Tracing paper.
4 Isometric paper, which is marked in triangles, for drawing hexagonal and other patterns, such as six-pointed stars, that are based on 60-degree triangles.
5 Heavy, quality paper for English patchwork.
6 Cardboard or mounting board.
7 Template plastic, including gridded, if available.
8 HB (semi-hard) and 2B (soft) graphite pencils.
9 Eraser.
10 Fine-point black ink drafting pen.
11 Compass with extension bar, for drawing extra-large circles and curves.
12 Protractor to measure angles and draft triangles.
13 Acrylic ruler at least 15 in. (38 cm) long × 2 in. (5 cm) wide.
14 Good-quality colored pencils.
15 Fiber-tip pens.
16 Metal ruler.
17 Paper scissors.
18 Craft knife.

Color value finders

Viewers are invaluable for evaluating color values during the design process. Use all or any of the following:

19 A reducing glass, which shows how your fabrics or quilt will look from a distance and how well the color values will work. You can get the same effect by looking through the wrong end of a pair of binoculars.
20 A multi-image lens—a Perspex (acrylic) sheet, through which you can see how one block will look when multiplied, and also how the quilt will look from a distance.
21 A value finder—a red lens that eliminates color but reveals value (that is, the relative dark and light tones). Note: the value finder is not effective when used with red fabrics.

Cutting tools

Good, sharp cutting tools are essential. Get your scissors sharpened regularly and never use your fabric scissors for cutting paper or cardboard. Rotary cutter blades need to be replaced regularly, although some firms offer a sharpening service.

1 Large fabric scissors. Look for a pair with spring-loaded handles, which are easier to use—especially if you have hand or wrist problems or want to avoid them.

2 Rotary cutter and mat—ideal for speedy cutting of patches and strips and trimming finished blocks. A useful average size of mat for general purposes is 17 × 23 in. (43 × 58 cm). Cutters come in various sizes, but the most commonly used has a 1¼-in. (3-cm) diameter blade.

3 Specialized acrylic ruler— 24 × 6 in. (60 × 15 cm) long—for use with rotary cutter and mat.

4 Acrylic square 12 × 12 in. (30 × 30 cm), for cutting squares of all sizes and squaring up blocks.

Templates and stencils

Templates and stencils are the master patterns for patchwork, appliqué, and quilting.

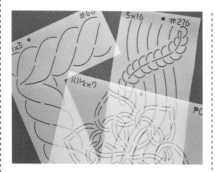

Examples of the different types of quilting stencils available.

Templates for appliqué

These can be drawn freehand or traced from patterns. Make them from cardboard or template plastic.

Templates for pieced patchwork

For hand-stitching, a line is drawn all around these templates onto the wrong side of the fabric to act as a guideline when stitching the patches together. Seam allowance is added as the fabric is cut, so leave enough space between shapes to allow for this.

Templates for patchwork

For machine-stitching, draw templates as for hand-stitching and mount them onto cardboard or plastic, then add ¼ in. (6 mm) seam allowance all around each piece before cutting them out.

A window template helps the quilter to place a design motif precisely in a patterned fabric.

Window templates

These enable you to frame a specific part of the fabric to position a motif. The inner shape is the finished patch size cut out to create a window. An outer frame of ¼ in. (6 mm) makes it possible to draw both the stitching and the cutting lines.

Quilting stencils

For elaborate quilting designs such as cables, shells, and feathers, you will need to use quilting stencils. These should be made of a durable material such as cardboard, plastic, or metal.

A selection of the types of measuring tools available.

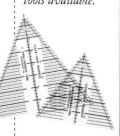

Sewing tools

You will need a good-quality sewing kit when quilting, whether you are quilting by hand or machine. Here are a few of the essential items.

1 Dressmaker's pins for holding small patches together, ready for sewing.

2 Long, glass-headed pins for securing larger patches.

3 Flat-headed (or flower-headed) pins for pinning patches that are to be machine-sewn together; they can be left in as you sew because they are specially fine and the machine needle can run over them without damage.

4 Extra-long, fine glass-headed pins for pinning quilt layers together.

5 Safety pins for sandwiching quilt layers together.

6 All-purpose needles in a variety of sizes for basting and hand sewing patches.

7 Specialized needles for hand quilting, called "betweens," which come in sizes from about 5 to 12, with 12 being the smallest and finest. Size 9 or 10 will be suitable for most purposes.

8 Good-quality machine sewing threads.

9 Quilting threads for hand quilting.

10 Basting thread.

11 Embroidery and metallic threads for embellishment.

12 Beeswax to prevent thread from knotting and to strengthen it when hand stitching.

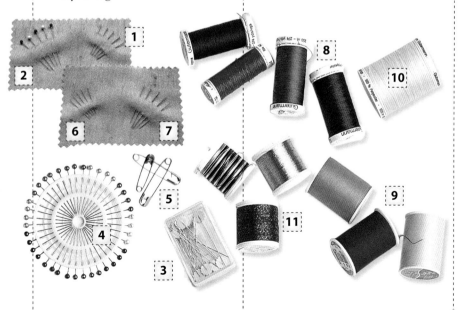

13 Metal thimble for sewing; thimbles with flattened crowns are good for hand quilting.

14 Finger guard (usually made of leather) for protecting the finger that is held underneath the quilt when hand quilting.

15 Small, sharp scissors for snipping machine threads and trimming corners; use them for small jobs to save your large fabric-cutting scissors from becoming blunt.

16 Seam ripper for unpicking stitches without damaging the fabric and for any job requiring a small, sharp point, such as holding down small patches while you are using a sewing machine.

17 Tape measure for measuring blocks, sashings, and so on; a metal tape measure is more accurate for large items such as finished quilts.

18 Hoops and frames in different sizes for holding the quilt for quilting; a floor frame will hold large quilts without the need for basting the layers together, if you have the space for it.

19 Fusible webbing that has adhesive on one side and paper on the other for holding appliqué patches in place, ready for sewing.

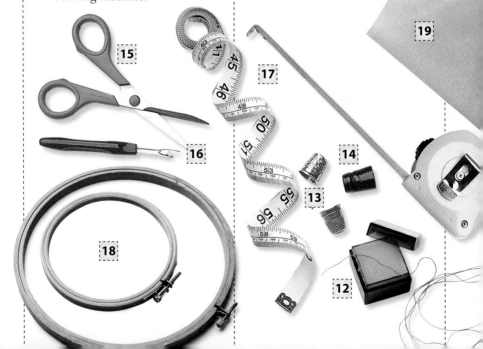

Fabric

Suitable fabrics for quilt-making include pure cotton in dress or light furnishing weight, lawn, poplin, and polycotton. Corduroy and needlecord can also be used, and their one-way pile, or nap, will give some interesting effects. A visit to a quilting supply store or search on the Internet will demonstrate the wide range of plain and patterned fabrics available to the aspiring quilt-maker. Study the small ads in a needlework or quilting magazine. Apart from fabrics for the top, a quilt must also have a filler, the warm interlining known as batting, and backing fabric to enclose it.

A value finder (see page 11) was used to determine that these fabrics are all the same tone. If all these fabrics were used together in a quilt, the design would look flat.

Patterns can be matched with each other if the scale of the pattern is similar, or they have colors in common but are tonally varied.

The selection below allows for the tonally dark fabric and the mid-tone patterned fabrics to be mixed and matched from block to block.

Backing

The backing on a quilt is usually a whole piece of fabric although "Back Art" is a recent movement toward making the back of the quilt worthy of attention. For a hand-quilted back choose soft cotton which will be easy to stitch through. Sheeting can be used for machine quilting. Stitches will be less visible on patterned fabric than on plain.
All fabrics used in a quilt should be similar in weight and fiber content. Using a thick, heavy fabric such as corduroy next to a fine lawn, for example, is not recommended.

Patterns can be matched if the scale of the patterns differs or if they are complementary colors (see page 24).

Adding colors that are nearly neutral to a palette can help a scheme with color or pattern extremes.

For hand-quilted pieces, choose a soft cotton backing; sheeting can be used for machine-stitched quilts.

Construction materials

The final appearance of a quilt and the ease with which it is quilted will depend very much on the "filling in your sandwich," i.e. the batting and stabilizer fabrics.

Batting

Batting is a very important part of the quilt and needs to be selected carefully. Many different materials are available to suit a quilt's purpose.

Polyester This is a man-made fiber available in different thicknesses known by weight, 2 oz (60 g) being the thinnest and progressing to the thicker weights of 4 oz (115 g), 6 oz (180 g), and 8 oz (220 g). This is the most economical filler. Choose 2 oz (60 g) for stitched quilting; the thicker ones are easier to tie-quilt.

Cotton This is available in two forms: pure cotton, which must be closely quilted or it will "migrate," that is move between the quilt top and backing and form lumps, and mixtures—one is called "Cotton Classic"—which contain some polyester and are easier to handle.

Domette This is a woven interlining. It is used to give wallhangings a flatter look that makes them hang well.

Needlepunch This is a polyester filler which has been flattened. Again, it is suitable for wallhangings.

Silk This is used to give a quilt or garment a luxury feel. It is rather expensive and perhaps best reserved for small projects using silk fabrics.

New products appear regularly so check the manufacturer's advertisements and Web sites. Sometimes you will see the term "low loft" with regard to batting. This means that the batting is a flatter one that gives a less puffy appearance to the quilt.

Various types of batting are available, each with different qualities and applications (clockwise from top: wool, cotton, and polyester).

Stabilizers

Stabilizing fabrics are commonly used in needlework for dressmaking and soft furnishings. Their uses in quiltmaking are less well-known, but when dealing with materials of different weights, different structures, and varying durability (such as silks of different quality, or open-weave fabrics such as cheesecloth, Indian cottons, or Osnaburg), they are invaluable.

UTILITY MATERIALS
All of these can provide a stabilizing effect within quilted work used for items such as placemats, purses, and millinery, as well as quilts.
• Muslin—available in different weights
• Buckram
• Canvas
• Calico or cheesecloth
• Insulating fabrics with thermal properties

Stabilizers for quilt-making
1 Iron-on interfacing
Available in different weights.
2 Quickscreen interfacing
Useful as a permanent foundation fabric.
3 Bonding web
Used for bonding fabrics when doing raw-edge appliqué. Available in different weights. Use baking parchment to protect your iron and ironing board cover.
4 Freezer paper
Used as a support for appliquéd motifs.

Other commonly used stabilizers are: Tear-away stabilizer (useful for foundation-pieced patchwork); water-soluble interfacing (for machine quilting/embroidery—it dissolves when immersed in water and is available for use in hot or cold water); heat-soluble interfacing (it disintegrates when heat is applied); heavyweight interfacing (used to mold three-dimensional shapes); and sheer gauze (for capturing decorative threads).

1 2 3 4

Designing a
Quilt

No two quilts are ever exactly the same. Whether you copy a design or carefully plan an original, the process of making a quilt has so many stages that you always have plenty of opportunity to revisit your design or fabric choice.

Designing with fabric

The obvious material you need for quilting is, of course, fabric, and there are some practical considerations to keep in mind. The first thing to consider is the purpose of the finished quilt. An item such as a bed quilt should be made from hard-wearing and fully washable fabrics. A purely decorative item such as a wall hanging, however, can be made from almost any type of fabric.

Types of fabric

The most useful type of fabric for patchwork is pure cotton. Cotton is washable and holds its shape well, and it is easy to stitch through several layers when quilting. It is also available in the widest range of colors and patterns. Cotton/ polyester blends can also be used, but they are more slippery to sew and tend to be more transparent than pure cotton. Many synthetic fabrics are too slippery and loosely woven for quilting, but firm varieties such as polyester silk can be sewn successfully.

Fabric grain

It is important to recognize the grain of the fabric when cutting out patches. Fabrics are made by weaving lengthwise and crosswise fibers together. The lengthwise grain runs parallel to the selvage (the finished edge). The crosswise grain runs perpendicular to this. A bias grain runs diagonally across the fabric (see page 44).

Cotton/polyester blends can be used but may be a little slippery to sew.

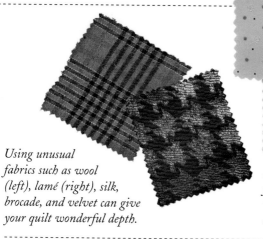

Using unusual fabrics such as wool (left), lamé (right), silk, brocade, and velvet can give your quilt wonderful depth.

Pure cotton fabrics are ideal for making quilts and come in a wide range of colors and patterns.

Color

One of the most fundamental skills involved in creating a successful quilt is the use of color. Some people seem to have more of an aptitude for color than others, but it is possible to learn how to use it to great effect by exploring the basic principles of color theory.

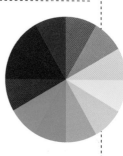

The color wheel

The relationship between different colors can be demonstrated on a color wheel showing the primary, secondary, and tertiary colors. The primary colors are red, yellow, and blue. Secondary colors are made by mixing two primary colors together, producing orange, green, and violet.

Tertiary colors are produced by mixing a primary color with the secondary color nearest to it on the wheel: red-orange, yellow-orange, yellow-green, blue-green, blue-violet, and red-violet.

Yellows *Greens* *Oranges* *Blues* *Reds* *Purples*

Color qualities

Colors that are opposite each other on the color wheel are said to be complementary—red and green or blue and orange, for example. They create vibrancy when placed next to each other. Colors that are close to each other on the color wheel, such as violet and blue or yellow and green, are said to be analogous and produce a more subtle and

Complementary colors such as red and green are opposite each other on the color wheel.

harmonious effect when combined. Adding a small amount of a complementary color to analogous colors will provide sparkle—adding a touch of yellow to blues and violets, for example.

Combining a color with colors that are midway around the color wheel, such as red with blue or yellow-green with blue-green, is known as a contrasting or clashing color scheme. This creates a discordant effect that can be dramatic but needs to be used with care.

Clashing colors such as brown and green can be successful if separated by a third color such as orange.

Analogous colors such as blues and violets are close to each other on the color wheel.

Patterned fabric

The next stage is to put your color theory into practice by choosing fabrics that will enhance the design of the block you wish to make. Patchwork fabrics are often produced in color-coordinated ranges that include solids, large and small prints, checks, stripes, and so on. If you want to give your quilt a coherent look, these fabrics can be a wonderful aid, and you can always supplement the range by adding some fabrics of your own choice.

Novelty fabrics are popular for children's quilts.

Most quilt fabric suppliers produce coordinated ranges of colors and patterns.

Small, medium, and large patterns add multiple colors and visual textures to a quilt.

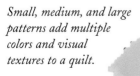

Solids and patterns

Quilt-makers have a wide variety of fabrics to choose from. Blocks can look striking when pieced entirely from solid fabrics, but take care that they do not become too stark. Patterns, such as stripes and checks, offer many design possibilities, and by careful placement, the simplest block can have an interesting visual effect. Fabrics with small all-over prints are ideal for adding texture to a quilt without being too distracting.

Medium and large prints can have a dramatic effect, and fabrics with large motifs are often used in center squares as a feature fabric. There are also plenty of novelty fabrics available that are ideal for center squares and corner posts.

Planning the quilt

Choosing fabrics is easy, but the selection should not be fixed until the design has been chosen. Quilts can be made up of one large piece of fabric with elaborate stitching or appliqué, or they can be made up of smaller repeated or individual blocks. It is surprising how much a design can be altered by the use of different fabrics and colors.

Start by sorting the fabric you have chosen into similar tonal values and then follow any directions the patterns may make about their placement (see Block directory, pages 122–175). Simply photocopy, photograph, or scan the pieces of fabrics and cut the shapes of the copied images out to match the design. Once your selection of fabrics and blocks looks good on paper, sew a sample block. Be critical, use a multi-image lens, or photocopy, photograph, or scan the block and cut and paste the image several times. At this stage, check that the balance of colors and fabrics is producing the vision you had in mind.

STAGES OF DESIGN
• Always start with the why and where of a quilt, and then consider how it will be used or displayed.
• Select blocks, fabrics, and colors for a harmonious design.
• Consider and map out settings and block placement.
• Decide and swatch methods of top stitching.
• Experiment with and think about border treatments.
Finally, and most importantly, at each stage don't forget, if necessary, to change the block design or any other element that was tentatively decided before. Of course, fabrics have to be bought and plans made but the quilt is not finished until the last border end is sewn in.

QUILTER'S WISDOM
• Use strips of colored paper between the paper blocks to design the settings and borders.

• Do not get too set on one block design too early. Try several—it may be that one block works better with your fabric choices and it may not be the one that seemed right when you were deciding on the design.

Patchwork blocks

Patchwork blocks all essentially break down into smaller units, i.e., four-patch, nine-patch etc. Many blocks have traditionally been made as 12-in. (30-cm) blocks since 12 is divisible by three and four. It is advisable to choose a block size that has the same ease of divisibility. Many people working patchwork by hand mark the sewing line and then judge the seam allowance by eye, but if you intend to use a sewing machine, an accurate cutting line including all seam allowances must be made.

Broken Pinwheel (Four-patch block, see page 124)

Wild Rose and Square (Five-patch block, see page 158)

Greek Cross (Seven-patch block, see page 160)

Stepping Stones (Nine-patch block, see page 128)

Compass Kaleidoscope (Eight-pointed star, see page 145)

Courthouse Steps (Log Cabin, see page 131)

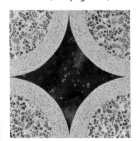

Broken Stone (Block with curves, see page 172)

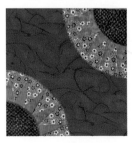

Snake Trail (Fan block, see page 174)

Mexican Rose (Applique block, see page 156)

Drafting blocks

Once the fabrics have been chosen, it is time to think about—
quite literally—the building blocks of the quilt: the blocks.

You can purchase ready-made templates for all sorts of
patchwork patterns, and sets of templates in different shapes
and sizes in quilting stores. These are convenient, time-saving,
and reliably accurate in their measurements. You can also
use computer drafting programs specifically for quilt-makers.
However, learning the basic techniques of how to draft blocks
yourself gives you great flexibility, not only
in drafting original patterns, but also
in adapting existing patterns to
whatever size you want.

*You can purchase ready-
made templates in many
different shapes and sizes.
Make sure you label them
clearly to avoid confusion.*

*Equipment for drafting
and designing templates.*

Square grids

Most patchwork blocks can be drafted on square grids. The conventional way of categorizing blocks is according to the type of grid used; for example, four-patch blocks are drafted on grids that are either 4 × 4 or multiples of four. This system makes drawing patterns easy once you've identified the category of the block. You can scale up or down to any size you want. However, not all blocks are drafted on square grids, so other types of grids are dealt with on the following pages. Follow this sequence when drafting on square grids:

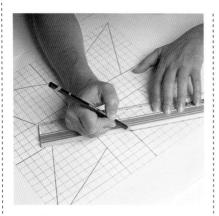

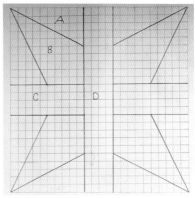

1 On drawing paper, draw a square (or other shape) of the size you want your block to be and draw a grid. You'll see that for each project that can be drafted on a grid of squares, the number of lines for the grid is given. For example, King David's Crown is a simple four-patch block needing a 24 × 24 grid. Draw in the lines of the pattern.

2 Use a black marking pen to go over the grid lines. Identify the different shapes in the block and mark them A, B, C, and so on. The diagram shows a simple four-patch block, but the method can be applied to any block.

Drafting geometric shapes

When drafting geometric shapes, first decide what size your finished block will be. The traditional size of a block is 12 × 12 in. (30 × 30 cm), but you can make it any size you like. You can use plain paper to draft your block diagram, but graph paper divided into ¹⁄₈-in. or 3 mm divisions will reduce the amount of measuring you have to do and therefore make the task easier. You will also find it best to use a set square and a very fine black ink pen because these will produce more accurate results.

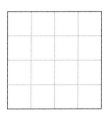

1 Draw a square of the size you want the block to be, then measure carefully and draw the lines for the grid—here, a 4 × 4 grid of 3-in. (7.5-cm) squares.

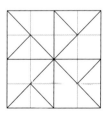

2 Draw in the lines for the block pattern. Identify the patches in the block.

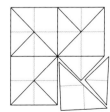

3 Cut out one example of each patch (if you want to keep your diagram intact, photocopy the patches onto another piece of paper and cut this). Use the patches as guides for making templates.

ENLARGING WITH A PHOTOCOPIER

If you use a photocopier to enlarge a block diagram, you will find that the more you enlarge it, the thicker the lines become, making it more difficult to achieve accurate templates. This is not a problem with appliqué designs, but pieced patterns require greater accuracy. One solution is to trace the enlarged diagram using a fine black ink pen, making sure that you draw consistently on either the outside or inside of the lines.

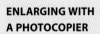

Eight-pointed star grid

Another grid that is used for some of the blocks in this book is an eight-pointed star grid, which makes it easy to draft a whole of stars (see pages 145, 166–167, 168, and 169). You can scan the grid shown below and use a computer drawing program to trace and scale it if you wish.

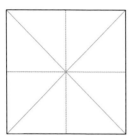

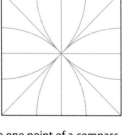

1 Draw a square at the size you want the block to be. Measure and divide the square diagonally, vertically, and horizontally.

2 Place one point of a compass at a corner of the square and extend the other point so that it reaches the center of the block. Draw an arc that extends to the edges of the square. Repeat this at each corner.

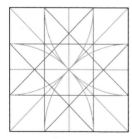

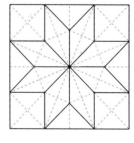

3 Draw straight lines that connect the ends of the arcs to complete the blades of the star.

4 To make the grid easier to use, trace the outer square and star shape using a fine black ink pen. Depending on the block you are making, you may also need to join various points on the star with dotted lines to created additional drafting points.

Drafting curves and circles

Lots of interesting curved-patch blocks and patterns can be drafted using a compass. Traditionally, circles and curves were drawn around whatever domestic items came easily to hand, such as plates, saucers, and cups of the appropriate sizes. You can still follow this method if you like, but there are some simple mathematical ways of drafting, which can be applied to several blocks.

The following instructions are for some of the basic designs used in the Block and quilt directory (see pages 122–181). To make the instructions clear, measurements are given for drafting to a specific size, but you can increase or decrease this size by adjusting the measurements proportionately. For this sort of design, you need good-quality drawing paper, pencils, a compass, a protractor, and a ruler. For curved seams that are to be pieced, you need to draw in a series of marks at regular intervals on the curve and transfer these marks to the templates. The marks are also marked on the patches to act as guides when you join the curves.

The tools below are used when making a block with curved seams.

To draft Robbing Peter to Pay Paul

The measurements given here are for a 6 × 6-in.
(15 × 15-cm) block. See page 151 for this block.

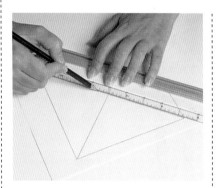

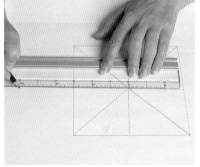

1 Draw an accurate 6-in. (15-cm)
square. Find the center by drawing
diagonal lines from corner to corner.

2 Draw lines through the center of
the square from side to side. (You will
need either a protractor or a ruler with
clearly marked right-angle lines on it
to do this.) Extend one of the lines
exactly 3 in. (7.5 cm) beyond the edge
of the square.

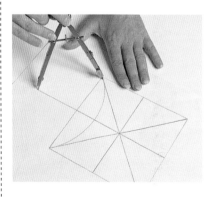

3 Place the point of your compass on
the end of the extended line. Open it
to 4 in. (10 cm) and draw an arc from
corner to corner of the square. This
arc is the template for the block. Trace
it and transfer it to cardboard or
template plastic. Remember, if you're
using the template for the fusible
webbing appliqué method (see page
85), you do not need to add a seam
allowance around the template.

To draft Drunkard's Path

The measurements given here are for a 6 × 6-in. (15 × 15-cm) block. See pages 132–133 for this block.

1 Draw an accurate 6-in. (15-cm) square. Place the compass point on the corner of the square and open the compass to 3 in. (7.5 cm). Draw an arc from one side of the square to the other.

2 Mark the curves of the design at regular intervals. (These are known as balance marks.) They must be transferred to the template, and then to the fabric. Match the balance marks as you pin and stitch the curve.

To draft an Orange Peel Petal

The measurements given here make a petal measuring 6 × 6 in. (15 × 15 cm). You need four petals for a 12-in. (30-cm) block. See page 149 for this block.

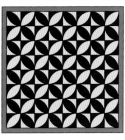

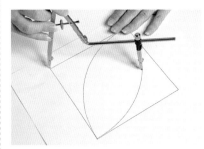

1 Draw an accurate 6-in. (15-cm) square.

2 Place the compass point on one corner of the block and open the compass to exactly 6 in. (15 cm). Draw an arc from corner to corner. Then place the compass point on the opposite corner and draw another arc from corner to corner.

Drafting non-geometric shapes

Some of the patterns in this book include patches with curves and irregular shapes. Smooth curves can be drawn with a compass, but you may find it easier to use a photocopier to enlarge the block diagrams supplied in this book. You can also use the following easy technique to enlarge them.

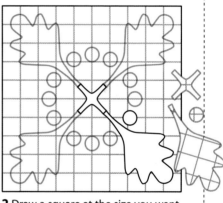

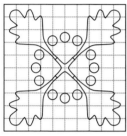

1 Draw a grid of equal-size squares over the original block diagram (photocopy the diagram if you do not want to mark the book). Use more squares for complicated designs, and fewer squares for easier ones.

2 Draw a square at the size you want the finished block to be, then divide it into the same number of grid squares that you have used on the original block diagram. Copy the main lines of the shape onto your enlarged grid, using the squares to help you see where the lines go. Cut out one example of each patch and use these to make templates.

Isometric grids

The most common alternative to the square grid is based on 60-degree diamonds. It is usually referred to as an isometric grid, and it is useful for drafting any pattern that involves 60-degree angles or multiples thereof. All hexagon patterns are based on this grid, as well as several others that you'll find in this book.

The following are some examples of patterns drafted on an isometric grid: Oriental Star, Right-angle Patchwork, Tumbling Blocks, and Six-pointed Star. Follow the lines on the grid to draw in the pattern. Use the method described above for making the templates.

Oriental Star

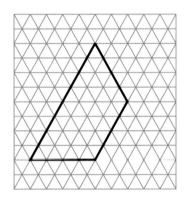

Right-angle Patchwork

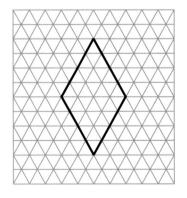

Tumbling Blocks

Six-pointed Star

Making templates

To make your templates, glue the patch shapes that you cut from your block diagram onto cardboard or template plastic. Add a ¹/₄-in. (6-mm) seam allowance all around each shape (use a quilter's quarter if you have one) and cut out on the line. Do not add seam allowances if you are making English patchwork and machine appliqué patterns. Use a craft knife if you are using thick cardboard for your templates. Mark the fabric grain line on the templates. This should run vertically and horizontally through the blocks.

QUILTER'S WISDOM

• Clear plastic templates are useful for positioning on patterned or pictorial fabrics.

• For a durable template, trace the patch using a spent ballpoint pen or blunt point, onto clear plastic sheet. Use plastic sheet available from a craft store or use the flat lid of a plastic fruit or vegetable container, soaking off the label first.

• Cut a small hole in the center of the template and cover with a strip of masking tape, to prevent the template from accidentally slipping. The tape can be replaced periodically.

At right are the tools you need when making templates.

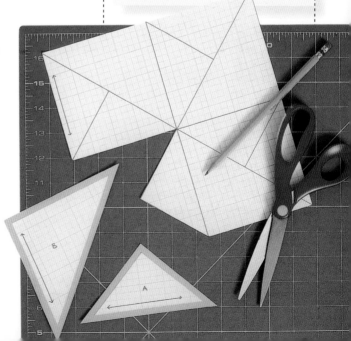

Settings and layouts

Some quilts place repeated blocks side by side, others need to be set with sashings—vertical and horizontal strips between blocks—to achieve their effect. Some need to be set on point, or diagonally.

Set straight edge to edge

Place two blocks right sides together, matching seams and points and sew in the usual way, using a $1/4$ in. (6 mm) seam allowance. Press the seam, then continue adding the remaining blocks until your quilt is complete.

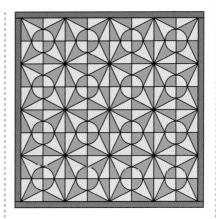

Alternate plain and patterned blocks

Alternating pieced or appliquéd blocks with plain ones is a great way of making a few patterned blocks go a long way. The plain areas of fabric also offer the ideal opportunity for interesting quilting patterns that enhance the whole quilt.

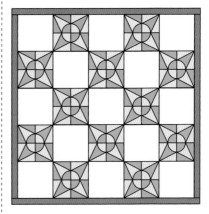

Sashings

Sashings are strips of fabric that separate individual blocks. Cut the sashing fabric into strips the same length as the block, adding seam allowances. Sew the strips and blocks together in columns. Press the columns and measure their length. Cut strips of sashing fabric of this length and join the columns, carefully matching the seamlines of the blocks.

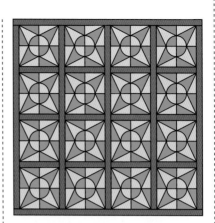

Sashings and posts

Posts are squares of fabric positioned at the points where the sashing strips meet. Join columns of blocks with short sashing strips as above, and cut more for the long sashings. Cut squares of fabric of the same width as the sashings. Stitch the sashings and posts together in strips. Sew the long strips and columns of blocks together, matching the seams of the posts and blocks.

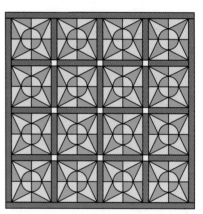

Set on point, edge to edge

Blocks can be set on point instead of straight so that they appear as diamonds rather than squares. To do this, stitch the blocks together in rows, but place the rows diagonally across the quilt. Plan how many blocks you need to sew together for each row, adding half and quarter blocks around the edges to complete the rows as necessary.

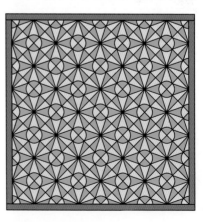

Borders

Not every quilt needs borders, but
they can often set off the blocks
and considerably enhance the quilt
top. There are several types of
borders: plain strips can be added
to the top, bottom, and sides, or the
strips can be finished with square
posts at the corners. Alternatively,
the corners can be mitered with a
diagonal seam at each corner, like a
picture frame. This useful technique
is also used in the construction of
some blocks, such as Chevrons (see
page 134).

*A border corner design
can echo a block design by
directly continuing either
the line of a seam or the
visual flow of the block.*

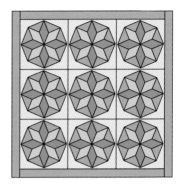

Plain borders

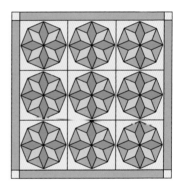

Borders with corner posts

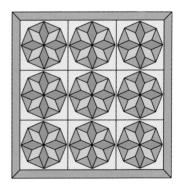

Mitred borders

Estimating material yardage

Unless you are making a scrap quilt from lots of different fabrics, it is important to calculate how much of each fabric you will need so that you have enough to complete the quilt. Sit down with a piece of paper and a pencil (a calculator and fat quarter or width of fabric are useful, too, especially when using templates).

Write it down

Decide on the finished length and width of your quilt. Calculate how many blocks there will be across and down the quilt. Next count how many of each block there are. Make a sample of each block and decide on your fabrics. Photocopy the pages of the book with your blocks on and stick your fabrics in place.

Make a list of all the pieces needed for each block and their colors. Then, working color by color, calculate how many of each piece you need. Quilt design programs, such as Electric Quilt or Quiltpro, can calculate the yardage for you, as well as make it easy to design blocks and quilts, and try different color schemes (see right).

Fat quarters

Fabric can be purchased in ready-cut pieces called fat quarters. These are half a yard of fabric cut in half, but in a fat rectangle, not a long thin one—that is, 20 × 18 in. The metric equivalent of a fat quarter is slightly larger, at 50 cm square.

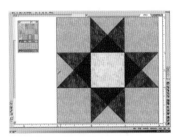

Individual block design

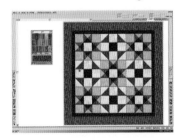

Quilt design

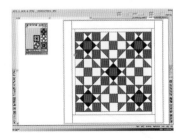

Alternative color scheme

Basic
Techniques

Basic techniques should be learned and mastered, but everyone has clever ideas and tricks that develop as tasks are repeated and confidence increases—try a new method if it works for you.

Preparing the fabric

Fabrics must be prepared before you can begin work.

Grain

Check the grain on a fabric before cutting into it. The lengthwise grain is known as the "warp" and runs down the length of the fabric; the crosswise grain is known as the "weft" and runs across the width of the fabric between the two selvages.

The warp and weft are the straight grain. Where stability is needed, items should always be cut on the straight grain, especially within patchwork.

Grain that runs diagonally across the width of the fabric (at an angle of approximately 45 degrees) is known as the "bias." Bias-cut fabric is very stretchy: once stretched, it won't spring back into place, so be careful where you use bias-cut edges. It is ideal for strips or patches of fabric that need to be manipulated around a curve.

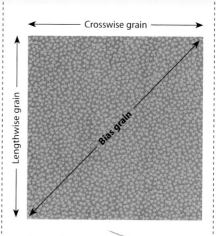

Crosswise grain

Lengthwise grain

Bias grain

PREWASHING FABRICS

• Prewash if you are unsure about the stability of a fabric (whether it has been preshrunk or not) and if you have any doubts about its colorfastness.

• If the quilt is to be laundered regularly, it is wise to prewash the fabrics to see how they behave in a washing machine at different temperatures. Once a fabric has been washed, it may need stretching back into shape.

• If you've prewashed fabrics and they feel flimsy, give them a new lease of life by adding spray starch when you press them. They'll feel good as new and be easier to handle.

Cutting into fabric

Before cutting into a length of fabric, remove the tightly woven selvages so that they don't distort the main body of the material. Iron out any creases.

If using rotary cutting equipment, large lengths of fabric can be folded to fit the cutting board. Up to eight layers of fabric can be cut into easily, but make sure you're using a sharp blade.

Mixing fibers

If you're using fabrics of various fiber types within a quilt project, take the time to stabilize the weaker ones with an iron-on interfacing or calico. This will ensure that all the fabrics are easy to handle and have more or less the same weight when it comes to the quilting process. It also makes the aftercare of the quilt easier.

REASONS NOT TO PREWASH FABRICS

- There's nothing as nice as the feel of brand new fabrics; they usually contain a dressing or starch, which makes them more resistant to creasing.
- Lack of opportunity. Short, one-day workshops held within a store usually involve using fabric straight off the shelf. In this situation, try to choose colors that won't be prone to dye loss, and opt for good-quality printed and closely woven fabrics.
- If you're using exotic fabrics such as metallics and silks, you may choose not to prewash those.
- Hand-dyed fabrics have usually been washed so many times in the dyeing process that they have no shrinkage left in them by the time they are used within a quilt. Be wary, though, of dyes that are notoriously difficult to set, such as reds and purples. Use a dye-catcher cloth in the washing machine and a cool temperature setting.

A cutting mat, a rotary cutter, and a ruler are essential for rotary cutting.

Cutting patches

It is important to cut patches accurately so that they fit together properly when you sew them. It is usually advisable to wash fabrics before using them, but especially if you are using dark colors that might bleed into lighter fabrics when they are washed. Iron the fabrics well, using spray starch to create a crisp finish. It will make accurate cutting much easier and the fabric will not fray.

Using scissors

Use a sharp pair of fabric scissors and keep them only for cutting fabric. Using them to cut cardboard or paper will blunt them quickly. If you are a beginner, mark and cut one piece of fabric at a time, but increase to several layers as you gain confidence.

1 Lay the templates on the fabric and draw around each shape, using a soft (B or 2B) pencil.

2 Cut around each shape on the drawn line, using fabric scissors.

Using a rotary cutter

If you are making a large project, a rotary cutter and self-healing mat make cutting patches a lot quicker and easier. They allow you to cut many different shapes and to cut up to eight layers at a time. Learning to cut accurately takes practice, so try your skills on scrap fabric first. Reverse the instructions if you are left-handed.

1 Fold and iron the fabric with selvages together, then place the fabric on the cutting mat with the fold toward you. You need to trim off a strip so that you have a straight edge from which to start cutting. To do this, align a small acrylic square with the folded edge, about 1 in. (2.5 cm) in from the edge you are going to cut. Place a long ruler against the left side of the square, matching its horizontal lines with those of the square.

2 Holding the long ruler firmly in place with your left hand, remove the small square and run a rotary cutter along the right side of the ruler. Cut away from you, not toward you. To keep the ruler in position on long cuts, stop the cutter occasionally and move your left hand up the ruler so that it is even with the cutter.

3 Measure the width of the patch and cut strips of fabric to this width by aligning the vertical line on the ruler with the cut edge of the fabric; for example, for a 4-in. (10-cm) strip, place the 4-in. (10-cm) line of the ruler even with the cut edge of the fabric.

4 Lay the template on the strip and draw around it with a pencil, then use the rotary cutter and ruler to cut along these lines. If you are using ready-made acrylic templates, you can cut directly around them using your rotary cutter, but cardboard or other plastic templates can easily be damaged if you do this.

Making basic shapes

Cutting strips

To cut a strip, place a horizontal line on the fold of the fabric and the line indicating your desired width along the cut edges. Keeping a horizontal line on the fold at all times will prevent you from cutting strips with V-shapes at the folds. When the ruler is in the correct position, hold the ruler in place with your hand—firmly splayed in the middle of your ruler—and cut with the blade against the ruler. Starting ahead of the fold, cut with an even pressure across the fabric. If you are going to subcut these strips, leave them folded.

Cutting squares

Place a horizontal line on the edge of the strip and the vertical line of the square measurement along the straightened end of the strip, and cut the square. You will have four in a stack.

Continue cutting the squares until you have the required number. If necessary, you may need to straighten the vertical edge again occasionally.

Subcutting into half-square triangles

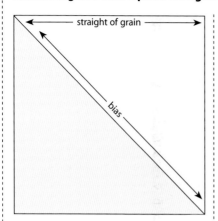

straight of grain

bias

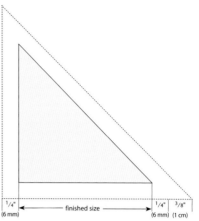

$^1/_4$" (6 mm) ← finished size → $^1/_4$" (6 mm) $^3/_8$" (1 cm)

1 A half-square triangle is illustrated above. It is used whenever the shorter edges of the triangle are parallel to the edge of the block or quilt.

2 To cut a half-square triangle, cut a square and then cut again diagonally. So that sufficient fabric is left for seam allowances, consider the triangle drawn on graph paper. Add $^1/_4$ in. (6 mm) all around, then measure the short side. It will be $^1/_2$ in. (1 cm) longer than the finished triangle. *Rule for half-square triangles:* finished size plus $^1/_2$ in. (1 cm).

3 Cut a strip the width of the finished size of the triangle plus $^1/_2$ in. (1 cm), and cut a square the same width.

4 Place the ruler across the diagonal of the square, and cut the stack of squares into two stacks of triangles. Repeat for more triangles.

Subcutting into quarter-square triangles

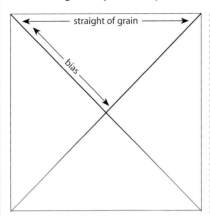

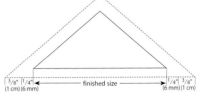

1 A quarter-square triangle is illustrated above.

2 To make a quarter-square triangle, cut a square and then cut again on both diagonals. To insure that sufficient fabric is allowed, look at the triangle drawn on graph paper. Add ¹/₄ in. (6 mm) all around, and then measure the long side. It will be 1¹/₄ in. (3 cm) longer than the finished triangle. *Rule for quarter-square triangles:* finished size plus 1¹/₄ in. (3 cm).

3 Cut a strip the width of the finished size of the triangle plus 1¹/₄ in. (3 cm) and then cut a square the same width.

4 Place the ruler across the diagonal and cut. *Do not* move the pieces.

5 Place the ruler across the other diagonal and cut. You will now have four stacks of quarter-square triangles. Repeat the process for more triangles.

Subcutting into diamonds

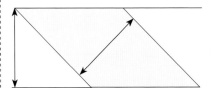

1 Diamonds either have 45-degree or 60-degree angles. The distance between the parallel sides is always equal. The strips that you cut are the same as the distance between the parallel sides plus the seam allowances.

2 When the strip is cut, you need to set up the angle of 45 degrees at one end by pivoting the ruler until the 45-degree line lies along the bottom edge.

3 To cut diamonds, keep the 45-degree line on the bottom edge, and slide the ruler across until the angled edge is on the line of the measurement of the strip.

4 To cut 60-degree diamonds, you should follow the same process. However, this time use the 60-degree line along the bottom edge of the strip.

Subcutting a 60-degree diamond into a hexagon

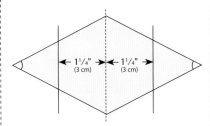

1¼"
(3 cm)

1¼"
(3 cm)

1 First cut the diamonds. Assume the measurement used is 2½ in. (6 cm).

2 To make a hexagon, cut the long points off. Cut half the original distance (1¼ in./3 cm) from the short diagonal. Make the same cut on the other side.

Speed piecing

Once you have mastered the rotary cutter there are many quilt patterns that can be cut and pieced quickly. For example the Log Cabin blocks can be made more efficiently if you can cut straight strips. Some quilt designs require you to sew the strips together before you cut.

Most patchwork blocks break down into simple shapes that can be cut with the rotary cutter. If a quilt is made of lots of repeated blocks, it is best to do the cutting for all the blocks at once rather than one at a time. Also, when a design calls for many half-square triangles, these are created using the "grid method" to save time.

2 Press the seams to one side —toward the center strip on one set and away from the center strip in the other. Matching the seams, place the two sets right sides together. Cut into strips equal to the width of the original strips cut.

Nine-patch block

1 Cut three equal dark and light strips. The width of each strip should be a third of the final block size plus a seam allowance along each long edge. Seam them together in two sets of three alternate strips—one set with two dark and one light strips, the second two light and one dark strips.

3 Arrange the desired nine patch and stitch. The final seams can be pressed open as desired.

Pinwheel and Broken Dishes

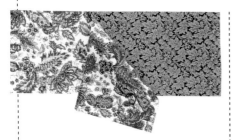

1 Cut two equal dark and light strips. The width of each strip should be half of the final block size plus a seam allowance along each long edge. Place the two strips right sides together. Cut into strips to create squares equal to the width of the original strips cut.

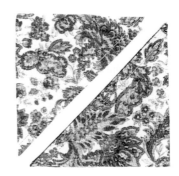

2 Place two squares right sides together. Mark one diagonal line on the wrong side of one of the fabric squares. Taking a seam allowance, sew either side of the line and then cut along the line.

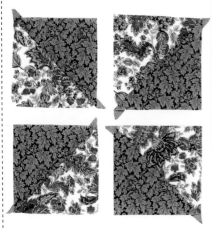

3 Press seams and arrange the resulting units in the desired block pattern.

Broken dishes

Pinwheel

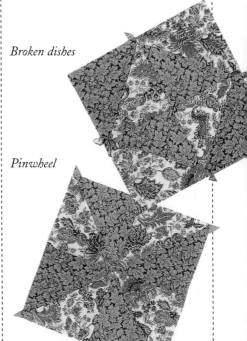

Making a block

Piecing order

It is important to ensure that all the patches are organized in the correct order before any stitching takes place.

1 When all the patches are cut out, spread them out on a flat surface in the correct position. Make up the squares.

2 Set the squares together in rows.

3 Join the rows to form one block.

Nancy Breland, *Mosaic* (detail)
*Accurate piecing of the blocks in the
quilt contribute to the complex
secondary designs.*

Basic stitching

Patchwork can be sewn by hand or by machine, although there are obvious advantages to machine sewing when you're working on a large project.

Hand stitching

A straightforward running stitch is used, except for English patchwork (see page 92). Use a fine, sharp needle and thread to match your fabric, or a neutral color if you are using a variety of fabric colors. Begin and end each seam exactly ¼ in. (6 mm) before the end; in other words, do not sew into the seam allowance. You may find it helpful at first to draw in the stitching line as a guide, marking a small dot where stitching begins and ends. Once you've made a few blocks using this method, you'll probably find that you can estimate the seam allowance accurately just by eye.

1 Make a small backstitch at the beginning and end of each seam and make evenly spaced running stitches along the seam allowance.

2 To join patches with matching seams, sew up to the marked dot and then pass the needle though to the next dot, without sewing into the seam allowances. This means that when you are ready to press the patchwork, you can press the seams in whichever direction you choose.

Machine stitching

A straight running stitch is all that's required to join patches and blocks by machine.

1 Check that the tension on your machine is even, and set the stitch length to between nine and 12 stitches to the inch (between five and eight stitches per centimeter).

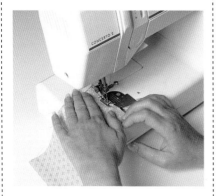

2 Lay the patches right sides together so that the edges are even. Stitch exactly ¹/₄ in. (6 mm) in from the edge.

3 Press the seams. Machine-stitched seams can either be pressed to one side, as in hand piecing, or open.

SEAM ALLOWANCE

An accurate seam allowance is important because if it is uneven the units of the block won't meet up neatly and your blocks may be of uneven sizes. Of course, you may wish to mark the seam allowance on each patch, but that's laborious when making a large project. Two alternative ways of getting an accurate seam allowance are:

• Use a special ¹/₄-in. (6-mm) foot, if your machine has one.
• Mark the throat plate of your machine so that you can see where to sew. Place a ruler under the machine needle and lower the needle so that it rests exactly on the ¹/₄-in. (6-mm) mark. With the ruler still in position, run a strip of masking tape alongside it. Place the edge of the fabric against the tape.
• Buy a magnetic seam marker. This device is placed on the throat plate to guide the edge of the fabric. Note that magnets should not be used with or near computerized machines.

Piecing angled shapes

When joining shapes that have angles other than 90 degrees—diamonds and triangles—align the stitching lines, *not* the cut edges. This makes a straight edge when the patches are opened.

Matching points

Many blocks have a point at which four or more different fabrics meet.

QUILTER'S WISDOM

Lightly spraying pieces with starch and pressing immediately before joining helps the blocks to stick together and prevents any slight pleating or stretching of the fabric pieces.

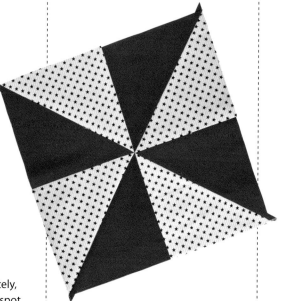

1 To match these points accurately, push a pin through at the exact spot where the points are to be matched, at a right angle to the stitching line. Stitch up to the pin.

2 Remove the pin carefully and then stitch over the point.

Stitching curves

Curved seams need care but can easily be mastered using the following method:

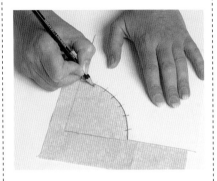

1 Make regular marks (balance marks) on the curves in the drafted pattern.

2 Transfer the marks on the templates to the fabric patches and match them as you ease the curve into position and pin it.

3 When you have finished stitching, snip tiny notches along the convex (outward) curves to make them lie flat. These should be not quite as deep as the seam allowance.

4 Press the seam gently from the back, then on the front.

Stitching set-in shapes

Most patches can be sewn with straight seams, but some blocks involve awkward angles and the patches have to be "set in" to the angle.

2 Stitch the piece to be set in along one edge, then pivot through the right angle and stitch along the other edge.

1 Stitch the first seam up to the 1/4-in. (6-mm) seam allowance to create the right angle.

3 Press the seam away from the set-in patch.

4 The finished unit seen from the front.

Pressing the block

For greater accuracy, finger-press each seam after you sew it by running a fingernail firmly along the seamline so that it lies in the right direction.

The general rule is to press the seam allowance toward the darker fabric so that it does not show through lighter patches. If too many seams join in one place, trim away some of the fabric to make it less bulky or press one seam in a different direction. You may also press the seam open if that works best. When you have finished the block, use an iron to press the block carefully from the back, taking care not to stretch the fabrics. Press down and then lift the iron to reposition it, rather than pushing it over the surface. Turn to the front and press again.

Be consistent with the direction each seam is pressed from block to block. It creates a smoother appearance and makes piecing the blocks together easier.

Once pressed, allow the block to cool completely before stacking on top of another block or storing.

Blocks

Quilting blocks come in all shapes and sizes. There is a block for every need, and the method by which they are joined is what holds the structure and design of the quilt together.

Patch blocks

Four-patch blocks

The most effective solution to a design problem is often the simplest, and the four-patch block has the virtue of simplicity built into its structure. The basic block is just what its name suggests: four equal-sized squares of fabric stitched together. To make the block more complex, these squares can be subdivided within the grid. The Pinwheel block has the squares divided into half-square triangles. The composition of the four-patch block for the Pinwheel pattern is shown in detail on these two pages.

There are dozens of other four-patch blocks, some of which become subdivided into 4 × 4 or even 8 × 8 equal divisions, but as long as it is possible to impose an equal 2 × 2 grid over a design, it is four-patch.

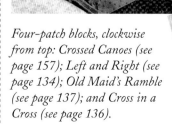

Four-patch blocks, clockwise from top: Crossed Canoes (see page 157); Left and Right (see page 134); Old Maid's Ramble (see page 137); and Cross in a Cross (see page 136).

Constructing a four-patch block

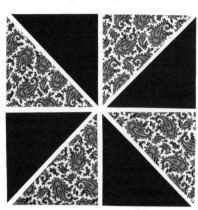

1 Place patches in the required position on a flat surface.

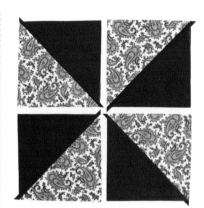

2 Join the triangles first to make four squares. Seams can be pressed open or to one side.

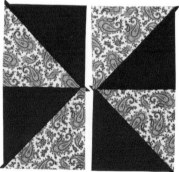

3 Next, join the squares to make two rectangles, matching the points.

4 Finally, join the two rectangles to make the square, matching the points at the center of the block.

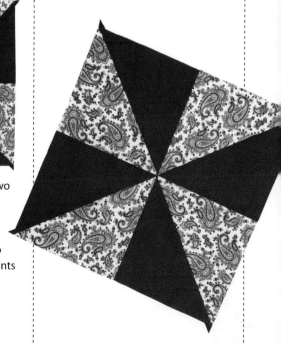

Nine-patch blocks

As its name suggests, the nine-patch block is divided into a 3 × 3 grid. The composition of the nine-patch block for the Shoofly pattern is shown in detail on these two pages. A vast variety of different designs can be created by dividing the grid in more complex ways, some presenting more of a challenge than others. Whatever your choice, plan the design with consideration of the tonal values of the fabrics to be used. Placing the emphasis on another part of a block can make it look completely different. Try shading the same block design in different tonal combinations. The results are often surprising.

Constructing a nine-patch block

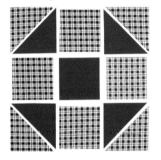

1 Arrange the patches in the required order on a flat surface.

2 Join the triangles to form squares. Press seams open or to the darker side.

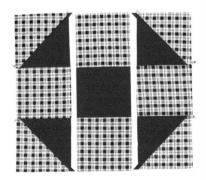

3 Stitch the squares into three rows as shown.

4 Stitch the three rows together to make up the block.

Irregular blocks

The whole area of block classification can be confusing when you start to study patchwork; even within the simpler categories of four- and nine-patch blocks, there is some overlap. For this reason the blocks which cannot easily be fitted into either of these sets are here termed as "irregular" blocks. By analyzing the shapes within the block, and determining the grid which fits over the block—whether it be equal units of 5 × 5, 7 × 7, or any other combination—it becomes clear how the pieces will fit together, and the block can be constructed. The same rules apply: combine smaller shapes to make larger ones, and sew in straight lines wherever this is possible.

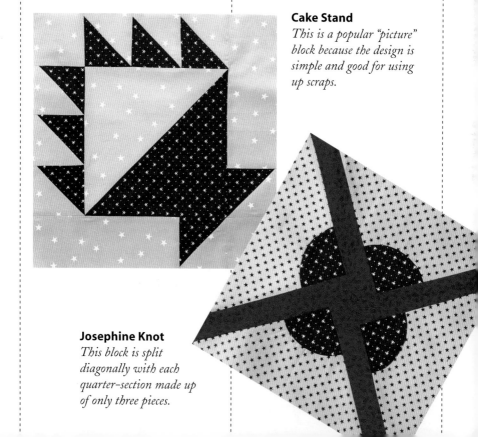

Cake Stand
This is a popular "picture" block because the design is simple and good for using up scraps.

Josephine Knot
This block is split diagonally with each quarter-section made up of only three pieces.

Log Cabin

Popular among the traditional designs, Log Cabin quilts are often seen to have a significance beyond their qualities of graphic design, representing home in the hostile conditions that faced the pioneers.

Although Log Cabin quilts were known to have been made in Europe, the design is largely associated with the early settlers in the United States, and it has maintained its popularity up to the present day. The construction of the Log Cabin block is straightforward; strips of fabric rotate around a center square, traditionally red to represent the fire or hearth. The block is split diagonally into light and dark fabrics to create the illusion of shadows and flickering firelight within the cabin. There are variations on this basic pattern, but they all rely on the visual play of light and dark tonal values. Although a single block appears simple, the versatility of the design can only be realized when the blocks are placed together in multiples, and their secondary designs become apparent. Dozens of different variations are possible, all with great visual impact and all of which exploit the contrast between the dark and light fabrics with graphic simplicity. There are many named designs such as Barn Raising, Courthouse Steps, and Sunshine and Shadow plus numerous others that can all be made by using combinations of the basic block.

The basic Log Cabin block.

Constructing a Log Cabin block

1 Cut a square of foundation fabric about 1¹/₂ in. (4 cm) larger than the desired finished size of the block. Press diagonal creases with a steam iron.

2 Place the center square, right side up, on the foundation square with the corners on the diagonal creases.

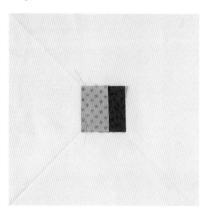

3 Sort out the fabrics into light and dark colors and cut the pieces, adding seam allowances. Cut a light fabric strip of the desired width and the length of one side of the center square. Place this right-side down on the center square. Pin and stitch through the three layers, taking a ¹/₄-in. (6 mm) seam allowance.

4 Turn the strip over to reveal the right side of the fabric, and then press flat against the foundation.

5 Turn the square through 90 degrees counterclockwise, and place the second strip right side down against the center and short edge of the first strip. Align the raw edges, then stitch down through all layers as before. Fold back and press.

6 Turn the foundation through another 90 degrees counterclockwise, then select a fabric from a contrasting, darker pile. Cut a strip, and stitch this to the block in the same way. Turn and press flat against the foundation.

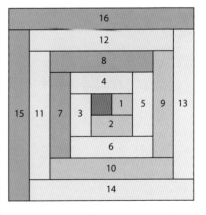

7 The fourth strip completes the first round. This will establish which is to be the dark side of the block and which is to be the light side.

8 Continue to add strips, maintaining the correct light/dark sequence until the block is complete. Trim away the foundation to the edges of the last round of strips, leaving 1/4-in. (6 mm) seam allowance all around, for joining the blocks together.

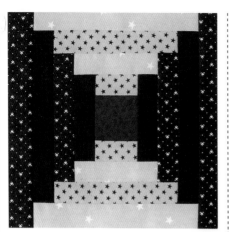

Courthouse Steps

In this variation strips are sewn on opposite sides of the center square in an alternate dark/light sequence, so a quite different effect is achieved. This pattern is sometimes also known as Chinese Lanterns.

Barn Raising

An arrangement of the blocks which results in concentric diamonds of alternating dark- and light-colored fabrics.

Sunshine and Shadow

The width of the strips can be varied. In this version the lighter colored strips are wider than the dark ones, giving the effect of curved lines. The Sunshine and Shadow design can also be made with strips of the same width.

Suffolk puffs

Also known as "yo-yo," this technique was used to make light bed throws from scrap fabrics in the 1920s and 1930s. Circles of fabric are gathered, and the thread is pulled up tightly to create medallion shapes. These are caught together at a point on each side, leaving spaces between which give a decorative, lace-like effect. The best fabric to use is fine lightweight cotton with a close weave, which does not easily fray and will allow the gathering thread to be pulled up tightly.

1 Decide on the size of the finished Suffolk puff unit and cut a circle of fabric twice this size. A piece 4$^1/_2$ in. (12 cm) in diameter will give a finished unit of 2$^1/_4$ in. (5.5 cm).

2 Turn a narrow single hem on the cut circle of fabric. An easy way to make an even hem on the fabric is to baste it over a circle of paper, turning the seam allowance over the paper in the same way as for English patchwork (see page 92). Press the fabric circle with the paper inside it, then remove the basting and paper. The turning will be firmly and evenly creased, and the circle will be the size of the paper shape.

3 Using thread to match the fabric, doubled if necessary to take the strain of pulling up the gathers, work a ring of running stitches around the outer edges of the circle. Leave a long knotted end at the beginning of the work.

4 When the circle of stitches is complete, pull the thread tightly from both ends to gather up the fabric. Make the opening as small as possible by pulling the gathers closely. Knot the thread ends together, and stitch them out of sight. Flatten the fabric circle with the opening in the center and steam-press. Make as many units as necessary for the project.

5 Join the units together with four or five whipstitches at a point on each side of the units, catching the folds together. Neaten the thread ends.

Biscuit patchwork

This rather novel method of patchwork makes a very light, warm form of cot or bed cover. Patches in multiples of a single shape, usually squares, are made into pockets and filled with batting. These individual pouches are then sewn together to create a textured surface of raised squares separated by the joining channels. No quilting is necessary as the separate areas are complete units that hold the batting in place and prevent it from migrating. Designs for biscuit quilts can be adapted from any traditional designs that are made up of squares; even a simple nine-patch is suitable. This would also be an ideal project for a scrap or charm quilt.

1 Each biscuit is made by sewing a larger top square onto a base. Preshrunk cotton in a light color is a suitable fabric for the base squares. Cut base squares to the desired measurement plus ½ in. (1.3 cm) for seam allowances. Cut the top squares 1 to 1½ in. (2.5 to 4 cm) larger than the base. A bigger difference in the size between the top square and the base will result in a fatter pouch, and thus a thicker overall quilt.

2 Place the larger square on top of the base, wrong sides facing, and pin the corners together. Then pleat the sides of the top square evenly, and stitch the two layers together on three sides by hand or machine. Stitch inside the seam allowance so that these stitches will be concealed when the biscuit units are joined together.

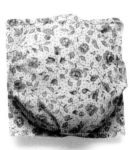

3 Push loose batting into the open side of each piece, using the same amount for each square. Pin the opening, and stitch the two layers together, pleating the top square in the same way as on the other three sides to enclose the batting.

4 Make enough units to complete your project. Stitch them together by hand or machine, taking $1/4$ in. (6 mm) seam allowance. Finger-press the seams open or to one side on the back. They should not be ironed as this may damage the batting.

5 To conceal the seams on the back, line the completed biscuit top with a piece of harmonizing fabric, finishing the edges with binding or by turning the edges together. The quilt top and backing fabric can be secured together with stitches or knots at regular intervals between the biscuit units.

Folded star patchwork

Rectangles of fabric folded into small triangles make these crisp star medallions, which can be incorporated into quilts or used as centers for cushions and smaller items. When selecting fabric for Folded Star, look for pure cotton that creases well, and choose a color scheme with sharp contrasts. Plain colors or small prints are the most effective; larger prints will not work as well when folded into small units. The medallions are worked from the center—each round of triangles is held down at the point and stitched to a foundation square. The folding and overlapping produces quite a thickness of fabric, so it is not practical to quilt it.

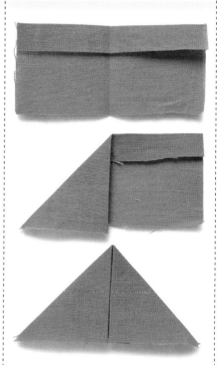

OVERCASTING

Overcasting is used to finish the edges of fabrics that fray easily. Work from either direction, taking the thread over the edge of the fabric with each stitch. Do not pull the thread too tightly, or the edges of the fabric will curl and make bulges.

1 Cut a square of foundation fabric larger than the finished size of the medallion by about 2 in. (5 cm) all around. To make the triangles, cut a strip of fabric 1¹/₂ in. (4 cm) wide across the fabric from selvage to selvage. Fold down a ¹/₄-in. (6-mm) hem along one long edge. Cut this strip into 2¹/₂-in. (6.5 cm) pieces. Fold these pieces in half to find the center, then fold the corners down to create triangles and steam-press.

2 *Round 1:* Press the foundation fabric to form creases vertically, horizontally, and diagonally and arrange the first four triangles as shown. Secure the points to the foundation with a stitch and, if the fabric frays easily, baste around the outer edge of the triangles. Trim off the corners.

3 *Round 2:* With contrasting fabric make eight triangles. Position the points ¹/₂ in. (1.3 cm) away from the center, and stitch to the foundation through the triangles on Round 1, catching the points down with a stitch and basting around the outer edges. Trim the corners.

4 *Round 3:* Make eight triangles to contrast with the previous round and position these ¹/₂ in. (1.3 cm) back from the points of Round 2. Stitch down the points and baste around the outer edges as before. Trim the corners.

5 *Round 4:* Make 16 triangles. Position eight of these ¹/₂ in. (1.3 cm) back from the points of Round 3, then place the other eight with points just touching the star points of Round 2 (see above). Stitch and trim as before. Repeat this step until the star is the desired size.

Cathedral window

This technique uses squares of folded fabric as a background to show off small "windows" of decorative fabric. The preparation of the background squares reduces them in size by just over half, so allow about 2¼ times the finished size of the foundation fabric. Try various fabrics—a striped background fabric gives an interesting effect, or contrast a patterned background with plain inserts.

By hand

1 Cut a square of foundation fabric and turn a small single hem (about ¼ in./ 6 mm) all round. Press flat. Fold the corners to the center, pin down, and press well to give a sharp crease.

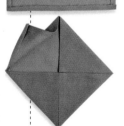

2 Repeat Step 1, folding corners to the center, then fasten these down through all layers with one or two small cross stitches.

By machine

1 Cut the square of foundation fabric, fold in half, and press. Stitch up the two short sides, taking a ¼-in. (6-mm) seam allowance. Clip the corners off the seams on the folded side and press seams open.

2 Pull the open edge apart so that the two seam ends meet.

3 Stitch across this opening, leaving a gap to turn the square through to the right side.

4 Clip the corners off this seam at each end, and press seams open. Turn right side out, poke out the corners, and press.

5 Fold the corners to the center and secure through all layers with cross stitches as for the hand-stitched method.

Joining the squares

1 Join as many squares as you need into a block. As squares are joined, the area into which the "window" will be stitched is created. This is a smaller square set as a diamond "on point." Measure this area and cut pieces of decorative fabric for inserts.

2 Pin the decorative panels in position and curl the folded edges over, then hem down in a smooth curve, using thread that matches the foundation.

3 Repeat until all the window spaces are filled. To fill the triangular shapes at the edges, fold the decorative squares in half diagonally, and pin them in position. Then hem the two curved edges down and slipstitch the folds together along the outer edge.

Crazy patchwork

The Crazy block uses shapes that fit together in an irregular but economical way. The jigsaw-like construction allowed for the use of every available scrap of fabric, wasting none of what was once a valuable resource.

By the last quarter of the nineteenth century the crazy quilt was transformed into a throw made of rich fabrics such as silk, velvet, and taffeta, and often embellished with sentimental mementoes, lavish embroidery, lace, and ribbons. The only similarity between these Victorian crazy quilts and their predecessors was their randomly cut shapes.

Crazy quilt patches are stitched onto squares of foundation fabric so no batting is necessary. There are various ways of constructing a block.

Method 1: Corner out

1 Start with a foundation square of white sheeting or similar weight fabric which measures 10 to 14 in. (25 to 35 cm) square. Position the first patch in one corner, and pin it down securely.

2 Work across from the corner, pinning down further pieces and overlapping the edges by about $1/4$ to $1/2$ in. (0.6 to 1.3 cm) to fit them together like a jigsaw.

LINEAR EDGING STITCHES

Herringbone stitch

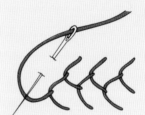

Feather stitch

Cross stitch

3 When the foundation is covered, turn under the raw edges and tack down the pieces to the foundation. Leave raw edges around the outside of the square – these will be contained by the seams when the blocks are joined together.

4 Embroider over the edges where the patches overlap. Ribbons and lace can be added to the patches. Trim the completed squares to the same size and join them together with a ¹/₄-in. (6-mm) seam allowance, stitching through all layers.

In crazy patchwork, linear stitches such as herringbone, feather, and cross stitch form attractive decoration to the seams. They also hold the patches down securely.

Method 2: Center out

In this method the block is built outward around a center patch. Prepare the foundation square as for Method 1 and select a piece of interesting fabric for the center patch.

1 Cut out a four-or five-sided shape, and put this right-side up in the center on top of the foundation. Press lightly and pin down.

2 Select a second fabric and cut a random straight-sided piece. Place this right-side down, aligning one straight edge against one side of the first patch. Stitch by hand or machine through the two layers and the foundation fabric, using a running stitch and taking $1/4$ in. (6 mm) seam allowance.

3 Flip patch 2 over to reveal the right side of the fabric and trim so that the straight edges of patch 1 extend along the edges of patch 2.

4 Add further patches right-side down along the straight edges created as you stitch and flip them over. Continue until the foundation square is completely covered. Trim the square and press.

The blocks can be joined edge to edge as illustrated here in Cat Crazy, *or separated with sashing strips.*

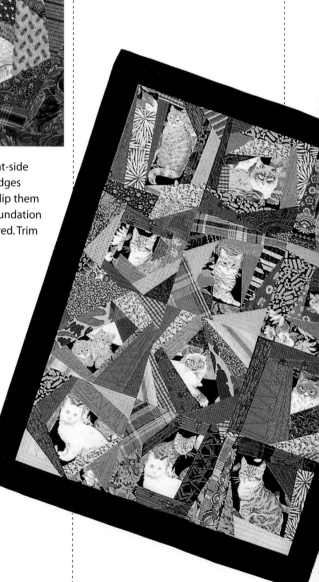

Appliqué quilts

If you have a sewing machine that will do an even, close satin stitch—the same stitch that is used for buttonholes—then you will be able to work appliqué panels by machine. The satin stitch is used to stitch down the shapes and cover the raw edges simultaneously, so no seam allowances are necessary. When designing panels for machine appliqué, begin with simple shapes that can be easily guided through the sewing machine without too many sharp turns. Flower, fruit, and leaf shapes can provide inspiration when designing appliqué panels.

1 When you have worked out a design, decide whether it is necessary to make templates; simple shapes may be cut freehand. Trace more complicated shapes from your drawing and make templates from thin cardboard.

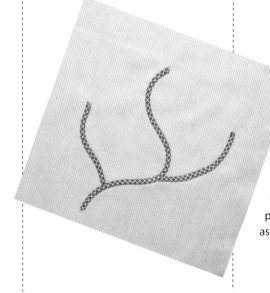

2 Cut a piece of fabric for the background slightly larger than the desired finished size, and begin by stitching the preliminary details such as stems using machine straight stitch. If you are adding appliqué to a patchwork block, you should assemble the patchwork block first.

3 Choose fabrics appropriate to your design, and press well to remove all creases. When stitching appliqué shapes by machine, the background has a tendency to pucker. To avoid this, use a paper-backed fusible web. Place this against the wrong side of the appliqué fabric with the glue side, which feels slightly rougher than the paper side, down. Iron to the fabric with a medium heat. Appliqué shapes can be drawn on paper freehand, or you can draw around templates made from your design. Cut out the appliqué shapes and the paper together (see above), then peel away the paper.

4 Position the appliqué shape onto the background and press with a medium iron to fuse. When all the appliqué shapes are in position, set the machine to the correct stitch. If you are *not* using paper-backed fusible web, stitch around the appliqué shape first with a straight stitch or open zigzag stitch to hold it, then set the stitch to a close satin stitch. Loosen the top tension slightly, to prevent the bottom thread from showing on the top. Guide the shapes through the machine, turning to follow the curves. If you can, vary the width of the zigzag as you go. Try narrowing it to a point for leaf tips, or widening it to make more rounded curves.

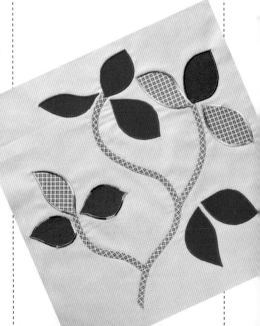

Variegated machine embroidery threads give an interesting effect around the edges of the appliqué shapes.

Hawaiian appliqué

Hawaiian appliqué is designed much in the same way that paper snowflakes are cut—the top fabric is folded and cut in layers. Hawaiian quilts are traditionally made in two bright plain colors, usually red or blue on white. The appliqué covers most of the background, which can be as big as a full-size bedspread or as small as a cushion. The quilting, known as "echo" or "wave" quilting, follows the shape of the appliqué and radiates out in lines rather like ripples across the background to the edges of the piece. In Hawaii this method of quilting is called "Luma Lau."

1 Try out folded paper designs before making a final choice. Fold paper squares in half, then into quarters, and finally into eighths. Draw and cut the design between the two folded edges, which should remain uncut. Open out the paper, and check the designs until you have a satisfactory one. Cut out a one-eighth segment to use as a template.

2 Cut two squares of fabric 2 in. (5 cm) or so larger than the paper pattern; one for the background and one for the appliqué. Fold each one in half and in half again, ironing the creases and making sure the grain runs straight with the folds. Finally, fold diagonally, pressing again. Pin the paper template onto the appliqué fabric, and mark around the shape. Remove the paper, and pin the fabric layers back together. Cut out the appliqué with a pair of sharp scissors, making sure that the layers do not shift.

3 Unfold the background fabric, and smooth it out on a flat surface. Remove the pins from the appliqué, unfold it and position it onto the background, lining up the creases and pinning the two layers together. Work from the center outward and smooth as you go. Baste all round the shape ¹/₄ in. (6 mm) from the edges.

4 Starting near the center and turning under the raw edges of the appliqué with the point of the needle as you go, slip-hem the appliqué shape, using thread to match. When there is a sharp inner turn, make several stitches to prevent fraying. To stitch points, work up to the tip, then tuck under the fabric on the other side with the needle and continue. Always use small, close stitches.

5 To quilt, assemble the top, batting, and backing and baste the three layers together. Quilt, echoing the shapes of the appliqué in lines about ¹/₂ in. (1.3 cm) apart.

Reverse appliqué

Reverse appliqué is done by placing two or more layers of fabric together, and then cutting away the upper layers in a design. When it is worked by hand, the raw edges of the fabric must be turned under to neaten them. Choose finely woven, pure cotton fabrics that will not easily fray for reverse appliqué; when turning the fabric under in curves and sharp inner corners, the fabric has to be clipped, and this may create a weak point at which a coarsely woven fabric will fray.

The same principles apply to reverse appliqué by machine or by hand: fabric is layered and stitched together, and the upper layers are cut away to reveal the design. The difference is that no turnings need to be made when sewing by machine, as the shapes are stitched together with a close satin stitch that holds down the fabrics and seals the raw edges simultaneously.

Hand reverse appliqué

1 Cut two pieces of fabric in the desired finished size of the work, allowing 1 in. (2.5 cm) extra around the outer edge for turning. Press them together, placing the right side of the lower fabric against the wrong side of the upper one. Draw the design onto the top fabric, then baste around the outer edge of it, just over 1/2 in. (1.3 cm) away.

2 Using a small, sharp pair of scissors, cut away the top fabric 1/4 in. (6 mm) inside the drawn line. Clip any concave curves and inner corners toward, and just inside, the drawn line.

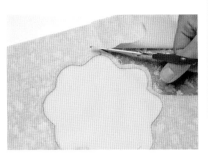

3 Select thread that matches the top fabric. Turning under the raw edges on the drawn line as you go, slipstitch the top layer of fabric to the one underneath. Use small, neat stitches and turn the edge under with the point of your needle, holding it in place with your thumb just ahead of your stitching. At sharp inner corners place two or three stitches close together to prevent fraying.

4 The edges of the two layers of fabric can be basted together around the outside of the piece, or trim excess fabric from the top layer $^1/_4$ in. (6 mm) away from your stitching if preferred. This will serve to reduce bulk on the finished piece.

6 More shapes can be added, building up the design from three or four colors. Press reverse appliqué on a thick pad such as a towel to prevent it from becoming too flattened.

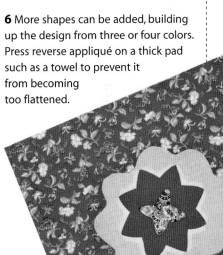

5 For a third color draw a second shape onto the appliqué fabric. Cut the third fabric slightly larger than this shape and pin it behind the drawing on the front. Baste around the drawing as in Step 1, then cut away the new shape and hem down. Use thread to match the second color.

Making the
Top Quilt

It is easy to get overwhelmed by the yards of fabric at this stage. Make one block at at time, try to keep your working methods consistent, and set a few easily achievable goals.

Hand block piecing

English patchwork

English patchwork, also known as mosaic patchwork, is a method of piecing patchwork over paper templates. The patches, which are made by basting fabric over the templates, are then hand stitched together by taking small stitches across the tops of the patches.

The advantage of this method of patchwork is that it makes it possible to handle fabrics like silk and satin because the paper anchors them while they are being sewn together. It also makes awkward angles easy—complicated geometric shapes can easily be fitted together just as in mosaic tiles.

1 Draw around your master templates on paper and cut out as many paper templates as you will need for each shape. The total number will depend on your particular project. If you need a lot of paper templates, you can cut out several at a time. Layer three or four papers together under the template, hold them firmly, and cut around the edge of the template.

2 Lay a paper template on a piece of fabric and pin it in place.

3 Cut out the fabric, leaving at least $1/4$ in. (6 mm) all around the template.

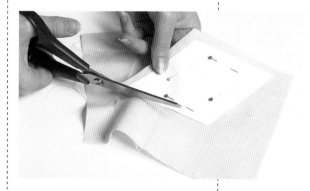

4 Fold the seam allowance over each edge of the paper and baste all around, folding in the fabric at the corners. Secure the corners by making a small backstitch each time you come to one.

5 Place the patches right sides together with the edges even. Make a knot in the thread and bring the thread through from the back so that the knot is hidden in the turning. Whipstitch the edges with small, neat stitches. Finish each seam by making a few backstitches and then snipping off the thread.

WHIPSTITCH

Whipstitch, also called oversewing, is used instead of slipstitch to join two folded edges of fabric when a strong joining is needed. It is an ideal stitch for joining patches together, see Step 5, left.

Thread a needle and place a small knot at the end. Working from right to left along an edge, pass the needle under the seam allowance of the front block so it emerges at the point of the fold. With the right sides of blocks facing and working always from back to front, pick up a few threads of the back pieces and the corresponding threads on the front pieces and draw the thread through. Repeat this at about 1/12 in. (2 mm) intervals along the seam. This produces a strong, flexible, and flat seam. Take care not to pierce the paper by taking too large a section of fabric, or to take too small a stitch and break the fabric threads.

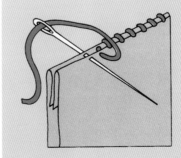

6 To fit a third patch into a tight angle, realign the patches and sew the first seam (see above). Instead of continuing with the same thread, finish off each seam with a few backstitches, snip off the thread, and start each seam again. You'll get a stronger seam this way.

7 When the patchwork is complete, take out the basting stitches, remove the paper patches, and press gently. If you take out the papers carefully, you can reuse them.

FREEZER PAPER
This is a waxy paper originally intended for food wrapping. The waxy side will stick to the back of fabric if heated with a dry iron. For an alternative method of creating an English patchwork-style quilt, cut out your template pieces from freezer paper and stick onto the back of the fabric. Allow the fabric to cool then cut the shapes from the fabric leaving a ¼ in. (6 mm) seam allowance. Turn the seam allowance to the wrong side over the freezer paper and press in place. Once all the pieces have been oversewn or whipstitched to their neighbor, peel the freezer paper away from the fabric. A pair of tweezers may help with this.

Adding borders to English patchwork
A different technique is needed for adding borders to English patchwork.

1 When you have removed the backing papers, leave the edges of the patches turned under and press them neatly (see left).

2 Cut border strips to the width and length required.

3 With right sides together, pin the border strips to the patchwork with the raw edge of the border strip even with the folded edge of the patchwork (see left).

4 Stitch, taking a narrow seam and stitching as close as possible to the junctions of the patches. Open the borders and press.

Joining the squares

Whichever way you have prepared the squares, the procedure is the same.

1 When you have prepared enough foundation squares, place them right sides together. Join along one edge with whipstitch (see page 93) from corner to corner.

QUILTER'S WISDOM

• Usually the same neutral-colored thread is used to seam an entire block—a thread color that could be hidden by the shadow created by the seam. However, because it is easier to change thread colors when hand sewing, you could use a small palette of threads.

• To make sewing easier, choose a short needle. It is quicker and easier to pass the needle through the fabric.

• Strengthen the thread by drawing it across a block of tailor's wax.

Machine block piecing

Chain piecing

Chain piecing is a quick way of sewing several sets of patches together. It saves thread, too.

1 Place a pile of pairs of patches with right sides together beside the sewing machine. Sew the first pair along the seam line. At the end of the seam, do not snip the thread but take another couple of stitches beyond the fabric. Feed in the next pair of patches.

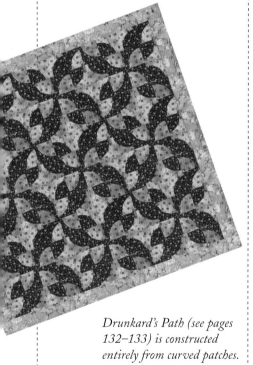

Drunkard's Path (see pages 132–133) is constructed entirely from curved patches.

2 When you have sewn all the patches, snip the threads to separate the pieced units and press them as usual.

String patchwork

This method of patchwork was devised to use up long strips of
fabric—perhaps offcuts from dressmaking projects—that seem too
narrow to be of any use at all. Seamed together and pressed flat, the
strips result in pieces of patchwork that can be used as a single fabric
to cut out the patches used to make up blocks.

Making a string patchwork block

1 Cut strips of the same length in
random widths between 1 and 3 in.
(2.5 and 7.5 cm). If necessary, strips can
be joined to increase lengths to that of
the longest piece. Don't try to keep the
strips of a consistent width; triangular
or wedge-shaped pieces give finished
blocks an interesting effect of movement.

2 Sew the strips together, using a
smaller stitch than normal to prevent
seams from coming undone when
patches are cut. Press seams to one side
on the back, and press again on the
right side to ensure there are no pleats
remaining. If necessary, stitch strips to
a foundation to stabilize flimsy fabrics.

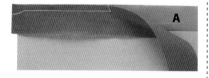

3 Place strip A right side up, aligning
raw edges with those of the foundation
fabric. Position the subsequent strips
face down against the preceding strip
and stitch through the three layers
taking ¼-in. (6-mm) seam allowance.
Flip the strip over and press against
the foundation. Continue until the
foundation fabric is covered.

4 When you have created enough
width to accommodate the template
for your chosen block, cut out the
patches and stitch the block together.

Seminole patchwork

The Seminole Indians of Florida devised this ingenious form of patchwork in the late nineteenth century. Long strips of fabric are first stitched together, then cut and reassembled into dozens of different designs. Plain, bright colors are the most effective, providing contrast between the characteristic small geometric shapes.

Approximately one-third of the cut width of the strips is lost when the finished design is pieced. Designs can be reversed, offset, or angled to give different effects.

Simple reversed designs using two colors

1 Cut two strips in contrasting colors, one 1 in. (2.5 cm) wide and the other 1³⁄₄ in. (4.5 cm) wide. Sew the two strips right sides together taking ¹⁄₄ in. (6 mm) seam allowance.

2 Press the seam to one side on the back, then press the right side. Cut into 1-in. (2.5-cm) sections across the strips.

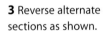

3 Reverse alternate sections as shown.

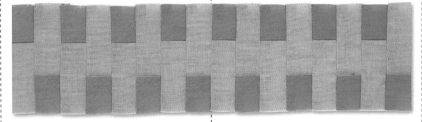

4 Stitch the sections together in this sequence.

Reversed design using three colors

1 Cut three strips in the following widths: 1$^1/_2$ in. (4 cm), $^3/_4$ in. (2 cm), and 2$^1/_4$ in. (5.5 cm), and seam together.

2 Cut across the strips in sections 1$^1/_2$ in. (4 cm) wide.

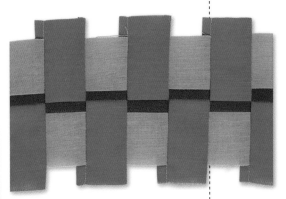

3 Reverse alternate sections and stitch back together, aligning the corners of the narrow strip as above.

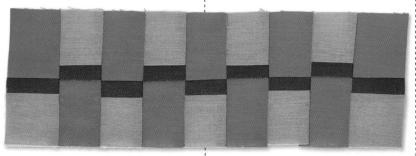

4 Trim away the excess fabric along the edges, as shown.

Angled design using two colors

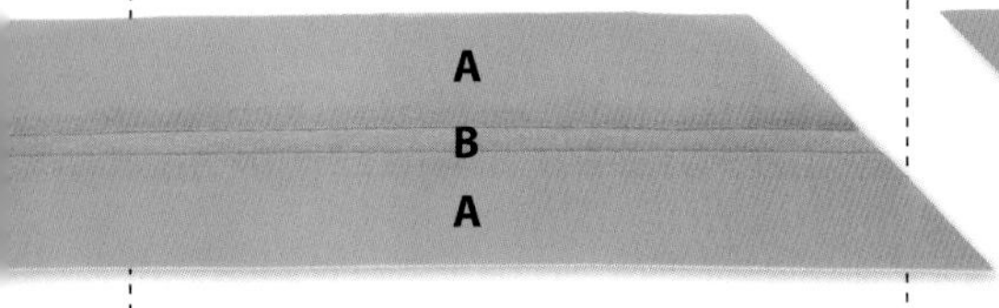

A
B
A

1 Cut the two colors of fabric into different widths as follows: fabric A—two strips of $1\frac{1}{2}$ in. (4 cm), fabric B—one strip of $\frac{3}{4}$ in. (2 cm). Seam together as illustrated. Straighten one short end, then measure 3 in. (7.5 cm) along from the top edge and cut at a slant.

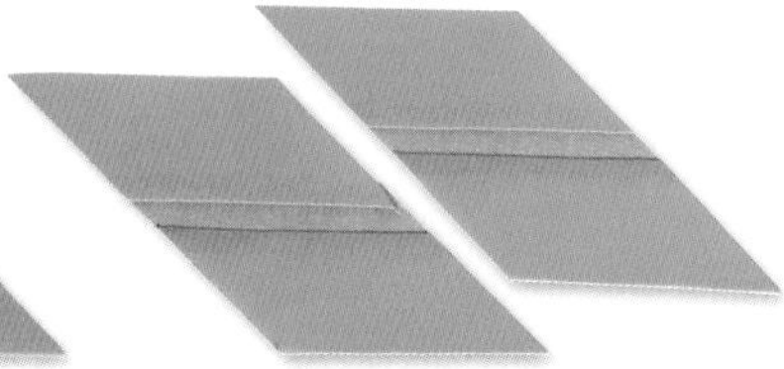

2 Cut 2-in. (5-cm) sections along the strip parallel with the angled edge that you cut in step 1.

3 Seam these back together. Align the strips as shown, offsetting each narrow strip by $\frac{1}{2}$ in. (1.3 cm).

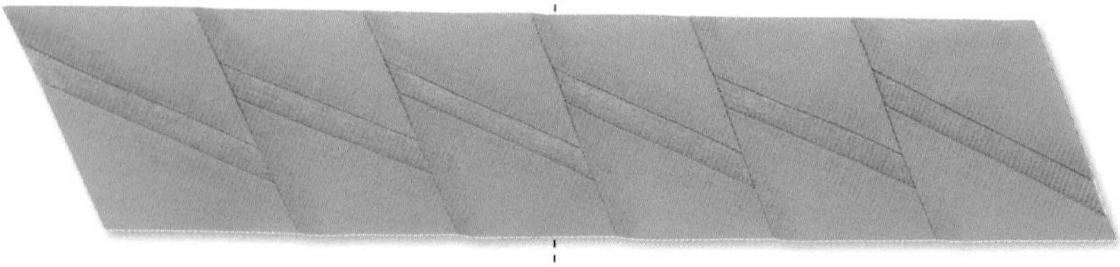

4 Press the seams and trim away the triangles at the sides, remembering to leave $\frac{1}{4}$ in. (6 mm) seam allowance.

Offset design using three colors

Cut two strips of fabric A, 1¹/₂ in. (4 cm) wide.
Cut two strips of fabric B, 1¹/₄ in. (3 cm) wide.
Cut one strip of fabric C, 1¹/₄ in. (3 cm) wide.

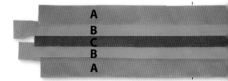

1 Stitch the strips together in the sequence illustrated. Press the seams to one side.

2 Cut into 1¹/₄ in. (3 cm) sections across the seams.

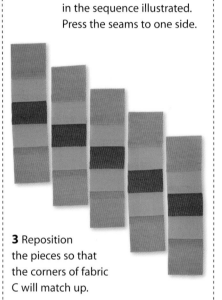

3 Reposition the pieces so that the corners of fabric C will match up.

4 Stitch the pieces together and press seams to one side.

5 Trim away the points at the sides of the length, leaving ¹/₄ in. (6 mm) beyond the corners of fabric A for seam allowance.

Sashings and borders

Sashings and borders can either be plain (of a single fabric) or have squares in a contrasting fabric, known as posts, where the strips meet. To add sashings and borders, you need extra fabric that complements the blocks in the quilt top. The sashings techniques shown on these pages also work for borders.

For plain sashings

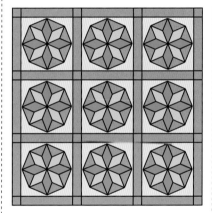

1 First decide on the width of the sashings, which should be in proportion to the size of the blocks. For example, a 3-in. (7.5-cm) sashing looks to scale on a standard 12-in. (30-cm) block. Each row of blocks is joined by strips the same length as the blocks. For example, use strips 12 in. (30 cm) long to join 12-in. (30-cm) blocks. Remember that the unfinished blocks will measure 12½ in. (31 cm), including the seam allowance, so that's the length you'll need to cut the sashing strips.

2 Work out how many sashing strips you need and cut that number. For example, to join three blocks you will need two strips plus one each for the beginning and end of the row, plus two strips for the top and bottom.

3 Place a sashing strip on the first block with right sides together, pin, and stitch.

4 Place the next sashing strip on the other side of the block, pin, and stitch. Continue in this way until all the rows of blocks have been joined. Press all seams away from the sashing.

5 Work out how many long sashing strips you will need. Measure the rows and cut strips to this length. You will need two additional strips—one for the top and one for the bottom.

For sashings with posts

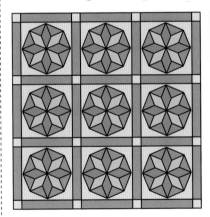

2 Cut squares exactly the same size as the width of the sashing strips.

1 Count the number of joining strips needed, including strips for the top and bottom of the quilt, in the same way as for plain sashings. Join the blocks in rows with sashing strips, adding one at each end of the row.

3 Make horizontal strips by joining squares and sashing strips, beginning and ending each row with a square. Join rows of blocks with strips. Add a row of strips and squares at the top and bottom.

Quilting and
Finishing

This stage is the icing on the cake, and like icing, can either be elaborate or simple. Do not be tempted to abandon your original test block design in favor of a simpler, quicker one—you may regret it later.

Preparation for quilting

When you have completed the quilt top and added any borders, the next stage is to prepare it for quilting and finishing. For this, you need a large flat surface on which to lay out the quilt. A large table is ideal, but if you don't have one, use the floor. If a quilting pattern is to be marked on the top, it must be done at this stage.

Quilting stitching methods

Contour quilting
Contour quilting involves quilting around each part of a design to outline it. Quilt around individual pieces of patchwork or appliquéd motifs.

Echo quilting
This method allows you to create exciting patterns by quilting around a patch or motif and then echoing the shape by stitching further lines that run parallel to it.

Quilting in the ditch
This is a method of adding puffiness to a quilt with stitching that does not detract from the design. To do it, work a straight stitch in the dead center of the seamline.

Infill stitching
Once appliqué motifs have been contour quilted, areas of background fabric can be quilted with infill stitching designs.

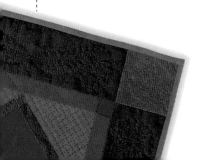

Borders and cornerstones
Borders can be quilted with the rest of the design, or they can be quilted separately. Long borders can provide an opportunity to use a long run of interesting designs such as cable, cable and feather, plaits, or vines. Cornerstones and setting squares within quilts can provide a good canvas for interesting square patterns.

Stenciling patterns

Patterns can be either stenciled on or traced from patterns.

1 Draw the pattern in black pen on good-quality drawing paper and fix it to a table or other flat surface with masking tape.

2 Place the quilt top over the pattern and anchor it with masking tape.

3 Trace or stencil the quilting pattern onto the quilt top, using either a soft pencil or a marker that can easily be removed. White quilt-marking pencils are good for marking dark fabrics. If the pattern doesn't show through, fix the pattern to a window with masking tape and fix the top over it.

Basting the quilt "sandwich"

If the quilt is to be set into a floor frame for quilting, no basting is needed. Otherwise, proceed as follows.

1 Measure the quilt top and cut both backing and batting at least 2 in. (5 cm) larger all around. Press the backing well and lay it out on the surface, right side down. Lay the batting on top of it and smooth it out carefully.

2 Lay the quilt top on top of the batting, right side up, and use long, glass-headed pins to pin it all over at regular intervals.

3 Using a large needle and a long thread, baste through all three layers (see above). Make big stitches and either work in a grid, or work outward diagonally from the center.

Quilting

There are several quilting options. Patterns can be used, or you can quilt a regular $^1/_4$ in. (6 mm) inside each patch—a method known as outline quilting. The quilt can also be finished by tying it at regular intervals with perle cotton or knitting wool (see page 109). For regular quilting, the choice is between hand or machine quilting.

Quilting by hand

The three layers of the quilt need to be kept under tension to prevent them from slipping apart. Most quilts can easily be quilted in a hoop. For really large ones, floor frames are available, but they need a lot of space. The advantage of using a floor frame is that you do not need to baste the quilt before you place it in the frame.

A good alternative is to use one of the extra-large hoops that are designed for this purpose. Place the hoop over one section of the quilt; when you have finished quilting that section, move the hoop to the next section. Continue like this until the quilting is complete.

The hand-quilting stitch is a simple running stitch. Note that the stitches must go through all three layers of the quilt and must be as even as possible. Evenness is more important than the size of the stitches.

1 Wear a thimble on the second finger of your right hand. Using a quilting needle (known as a "between") and quilting thread, make a knot in the thread. Bring the thread up from the back of the quilt to the surface, gently pulling the knot into the batting. Make a small backstitch.

2 Begin quilting by pushing the needle through all three layers, keeping the needle as straight as possible. Keep your left hand under the place where you're working and use your finger to gently push the fabric up just in front of the needle. You should feel the point of the needle at each stitch.

3 Make several stitches before pulling the thread through. Aim for a light rocking motion with the needle. This is best achieved by lodging the needle against the rim of the thimble.

4 At the end of the thread, make a knot in it and make a small backstitch. Push the needle into the batting and bring it out a short distance away. Pull the thread gently until the knot pops into the backing. Snip off the thread closely.

Tying a quilt

This is a quick and easy way of anchoring the layers of a quilt.

1 Use a long needle and strong thread, such as coton à broder or embroidery silk.

2 Pass the needle through all three layers, leaving a tail of about 2 in. (5 cm) on the top. Bring the needle back to the top very close to where it went in.

3 Make another stitch like this and snip off, again leaving a tail.

4 Tie the ends together in a knot and snip off the ends to about 1 in. (2.5 cm) or less.

Quilting by machine

Machine quilting makes the task much quicker than hand quilting, but it's advisable to practice the techniques before you embark on a large project.

There are two basic types of machine quilting: straight machine quilting, for any patterns that can be stitched in straight lines or gentle curves, and free machine quilting for patterns with more exaggerated curves.

Straight machine quilting

1 Before you begin, make a practice piece. Attach an even-feed foot or walking foot. Use no. 80 machine needles and good-quality machine thread.

2 Check that the tension is correct (check back and front) and that the fabric isn't puckering up. Quilt across the first lines to make squares and, again, check for puckering and dragging. Adjust the tension and stitch length until you're happy with the result.

4 Place your hands on either side of the portion to be quilted and press down gently but firmly. Soft cotton gardening gloves with small rubber grippers make it easy to hold onto the quilt as you work.

3 Place the portion of the quilt to be quilted under the needle. If necessary, roll up one section of the quilt and secure it with clips.

5 Start and end each row with a couple of backstitches. When stitching is complete, thread the ends through a needle, draw them through the fabric layers, and bring them up at the back of the quilt. Tie off and snip.

This stippling pattern is stitched using the free machine method.

Free machine quilting

Quilting patterns can be either marked on the quilt surface or drawn on tracing paper that is pinned to the surface and torn away when quilting is finished.

1 For free machine quilting, either drop the feed dog or cover it with a special plate, depending on your machine.

2 Fit a darning foot, or a special quilting foot if your machine has one. Set the needle length to 0 and lower the tension slightly. Make some samples, as learning to control the speed and movement of the work requires practice.

3 Begin by making a single stitch while turning the wheel manually, then bring the thread from the bobbin up to the top. This will insure it doesn't snarl up as you begin stitching.

4 Run the machine at a slightly slower rate than for ordinary sewing. Because the feed dog is disconnected, you must manually move the quilt under the needle. Move it as evenly and steadily as possible. Instead of marking the quilting design directly onto the quilt, draw it on tracing paper, pin the tracing paper to the quilt top, and stitch through the paper. Tear away the paper when you have finished quilting.

5 Meander, or stippling, quilting is done by moving the quilt under the needle to make random patterns. This needs some practice but is such a useful technique that it's well worth spending some time to master it.

Quilting techniques

Sashiko

Sashiko is a form of quilting that originated in Japan as a plain running stitch to strengthen or repair fabric, either padded or unpadded. The resulting fabric was put to a variety of uses, notably in firemen's clothing (which would be drenched with water before firefighting), and in clothing and household furnishings. Decorative sashiko stitching developed during the eighteenth century and was used for embellishing kimonos, hangings, and futon covers. The stitches are longer than a normal quilting stitch, and are done in a thread which contrasts with the cloth—black on white, or white on a blue or red ground and vice versa, are popular Japanese colors.

1 Start by working a square or rectangular panel of about 8 to 10 in. (20 to 25 cm). A geometric design using straight lines would be a good starting project. Draw it full size on graph paper (either squared or isometric), then transfer to the fabric, using dressmaker's carbon paper.

2 Assemble the layers. For preference, use a flat, low-loft batting; too much thickness will be difficult to stitch through.

4 Try to achieve evenness in the stitches. The sashiko stitch is traditionally longer than stitches used for other quilting.

3 Begin with a knot concealed between the layers, and try as far as possible to work continuous lines of stitching, which avoids breaking the thread too often.

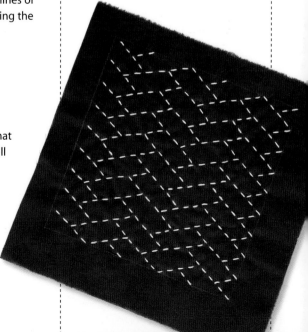

5 A thicker thread such as coton perlé no. 3, in a color that contrasts with the ground, will give a good definition.

Trapunto

In the technique of trapunto, the top layer of the quilt or wall hanging is lined, and selected areas are outlined with running stitch. Batting is pushed into these areas from the back to emphasize them, and make them stand out more distinctly. Trapunto can be combined successfully with other forms of quilting. It is very effective with a closely quilted background, or with linear details added in Italian quilting.

It was used to decorate clothing in the seventeenth and eighteenth centuries, and as a way of embellishing quilts, thus showing off the skills of the maker. Designs for trapunto should be made up of small areas that can be outlined individually. Fruit, foliage, and flower shapes can all be simplified, and used as a basis for trapunto designs.

1 When you have worked out a satisfactory design, transfer it onto the top fabric. A pale-colored fabric with a slight glaze will show off the trapunto best, reflecting the light and emphasizing the sculptured effect. Baste the top fabric to the backing, which should be fairly soft and loosely woven. Calico or mull are both suitable fabrics.

2 Stitch around each of the shapes in the design by hand or machine using a small running stitch. Finish thread ends neatly. Make a small slit in the back of each of the shapes, and gently insert wisps of batting, using a tool such as a knitting needle or tapestry needle with a blunt end. If the fabric has a loose enough weave, you may be able to separate the threads, and make an opening wide enough to insert batting without cutting the backing.

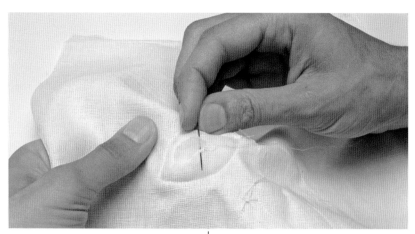

3 When the area has enough batting pushed up to the stitching line, either stitch the gap with the edges just meeting, or rearrange the threads to close it. Do not pull the stitches too tightly, as this may pucker the background. If you are combining the technique with Italian quilting (see page 116), work the cording at this stage as well.

4 The piece can then be treated as a normal quilt top and assembled with the backing and batting for further quilting.

Italian quilting

Wool or cord threaded through stitched channels forms a raised, linear design in the technique of Italian or corded quilting. It was used as a form of decoration on quilts and clothing as early as the seventeenth and eighteenth centuries and enjoyed a revival in the 1930s and 1940s. Corded quilting is more decorative than practical; it cannot be padded and this is one possible explanation of its name—Italian quilting—where warmer bedcovers were not as necessary in the Mediterranean climate. Light-colored fabrics are most suitable for projects in Italian quilting as they show off the sculptured effect more easily. Designs can be adapted from various sources; plant forms, Celtic knots, hearts, and circles, for example, could all be starting points.

1 Plan your design, and make the necessary templates. Cut a piece of the top fabric, allowing extra for turnings. The fabric for the back should have a loose weave, such as calico. Cut a piece the same size as the top and smooth them together, then baste them to prevent the layers from shifting. Mark the design on the top fabric.

2 Stitch along the marked lines by hand or machine in double channels, a scant ¹/₄ in. (6 mm) apart. If sewing by hand, use a running stitch or backstitch. If sewing by machine, use a medium stitch. If the design has lines that cross each other, decide which will be a continuous line, and stop the intersecting lines of stitching at the point where they cross each other, so the cord can be threaded through.

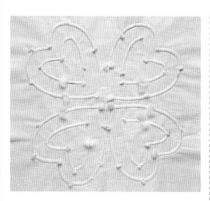

3 Thread a blunt needle with a length of quilting wool, and insert the needle into the stitched channel, pushing it between the backing fabric and the top fabric. Slide the needle along as far as possible, then bring it out and pull gently. Reinsert the needle through the same opening and continue, leaving a loop at the point of exit so that the wool lies smoothly on curves and angles. At the end of the length, bring the needle out, and cut off the wool leaving ¹/₄ in. (6 mm). If the design is circular, starting and finishing at the same point, stitch the two ends together to prevent them from disappearing into the channel.

WHOLECLOTH QUILTS
Italian or corded quilting has often featured on quilts made throughout Europe, as well as in Asia and the Middle East. The wholecloth quilt detail illustrated below uses Italian quilting to provide intricate decoration and relief. The designs of wholecloth quilts are characteristically inspired by everyday objects, such as feathers, shells, fans or, as in this case, flowers and leaves. The use of the same color thread for the quilting as the background fabric is also typical of wholecloth quilting, and contributes to its simple, traditional quality.

4 Completed panel of corded quilting, using simple heart-shaped motifs.

Finishing the quilt

When you have completed the quilting and removed the basting stitches, finish the edges by binding them or by turning them in—a technique known as butting. Alternatively, the backing can be folded over to the front, turned under, and hemmed down. Of course, this option is only possible if you've left sufficient excess of backing on all sides.

Binding edges

In this method, separate strips of fabric make the binding.

1 Measure the width of the quilt and cut 3-in. (7.5-cm) wide strips to that length.

2 Fold each strip in half lengthwise, wrong sides together, and press.

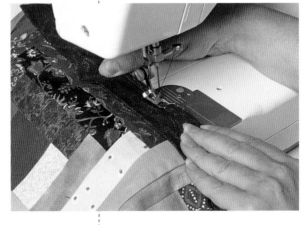

3 With right sides together and lining up the raw edges, pin and stitch the strips to the top and bottom of the quilt.

4 Starting from the middle of the edge, turn the strips to the back and pin the binding to the backing fabric. Hem the fold edge to the backing fabric.

5 Measure the length of the quilt and cut 3-in. (7.5-cm) wide strips to that length, adding enough extra length to turn under at the ends. Fold in half lengthwise and press. Pin and stitch the strips to the sides of the quilt, turn to the back, and hem them down, turning in the ends of the strips.

Butting edges

In this method, the edges of the quilt top and backing are butted together so that there is no separate binding.

1 Turn the quilt top over the batting by at least ¹/₄ in. (6 mm) and baste it in place.

2 Turn in the backing along the edge of the quilt top with the raw edge folded under. Baste again.

3 Finish by slipstitching the two edges together.

Self-binding

In this method, the backing is folded over to the front of the quilt to form a binding. This provides visual continuity between the back and front of the quilt and is an easy way to finish the edges, provided you've left sufficient extra backing fabric to bring it over to the front of the quilt.

1 Trim off the excess batting so that it is level with the quilt top.

2 Fold the backing fabric over so that the raw edge is level with the quilt top.

3 Fold the backing fabric over again, then working from the center outward, pin it to the front of the quilt.

4 Baste into position.

5 Working from right to left along an edge with the edge facing, hem with invisible stitches (see Quilter's wisdom at right).

QUILTER'S WISDOM
For a stronger seam, insert the needle through the fold of the binding and slide it along to emerge $^1/_8$ in. (3 mm) farther along the fold. Insert the needle under the quilt top immediately opposite where the needle emerged and slide it along to emerge $^1/_8$ in. (3 mm) further along the front. Repeat to the end.

Block and
Quilt Directory

In this chapter you will find patterns for over 40 block designs. In addition, a number of quilting techniques are featured, giving you everything you need to create beautiful and original quilts.

Broken Pinwheel

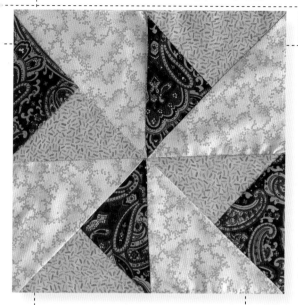

Pinwheel blocks always look effective, even as scrap quilts. A light fabric has been used for the large triangles in this block, but you could choose a dark fabric instead, with medium and light fabrics for the two smaller triangles. The two smaller triangles could also be made using two medium-shaded fabrics, as long as there is a good contrast between them.

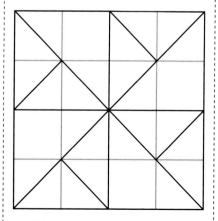

Drafting

Draft the block on a 4 × 4 grid and make the templates.

Cutting guide

Cut out all the fabric in the required shapes as directed.

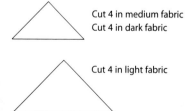

Cut 4 in medium fabric
Cut 4 in dark fabric

Cut 4 in light fabric

Pinwheel quilting patterns

"Pinwheel" is a patchwork block designed on a 2 × 2 grid (four squares in total). With careful fabric placement an optical illusion of movement can be achieved, making it look like a rotating windmill. Quilting designs can be simple, such as quilting in the ditch, or contour-quilting around the individual patches.

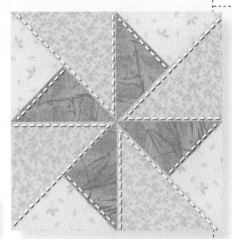

Contour quilting

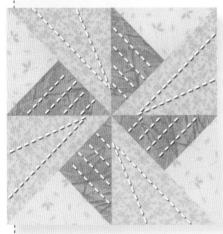

Geometric design: echoing movement

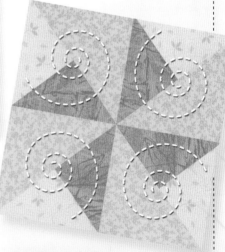

Curvilinear design: quartered spirals

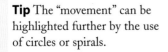

Tip The "movement" can be highlighted further by the use of circles or spirals.

Flock of Geese

Flock of Geese is one of many similar patterns based on the shapes made by birds in flight. Geese do fly in a V-formation, when they are described as a "skein of geese," but old-time quilt-makers were never pedantic. This is a very easy block, but because the colors on either side of the long diagonal are not symmetrical, it has interesting design possibilities.

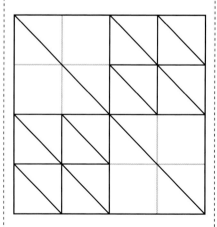

Drafting

Draft the block on a 4 × 4 grid and make the templates.

Cutting guide

Cut out all the fabric in the required shapes as directed.

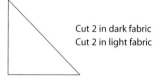

Cut 2 in dark fabric
Cut 2 in light fabric

Cut 8 in dark fabric
Cut 8 in light fabric

Butterfly at the Crossroads

Butterfly at the Crossroads is another of the many blocks in which the name is an imaginative interpretation of the shapes within it. It is a versatile block that, with some minor amendments, can be transformed into other five-patch blocks.

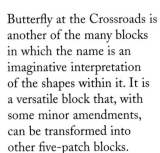

Drafting

Draft the block on a 5 × 5 grid and make the templates.

Cutting guide

Cut out all the fabric in the required shapes as directed.

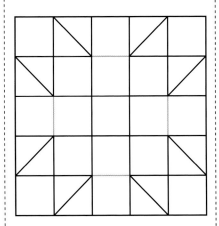

Cut 4 in light fabric
Cut 5 in dark fabric

Cut 8 in light fabric
Cut 8 in dark fabric

Cut 4 in light fabric

Stepping Stones

This is but one of many variations on the very old Jacob's Ladder block. The striking graphic impact depends on the use of fabrics with a strong light/dark contrast, which results in a series of stripes running across the quilt. Interesting patterns emerge when repeated blocks are rotated, making this an excellent scrap quilt, provided the color contrasts are strong.

Cutting guide

Cut out all the fabric in the required shapes as directed.

Cut 4 in dark fabric
Cut 4 in medium fabric

Cut 10 in dark fabric
Cut 10 in light fabric

Drafting

Draft the block on a 6 × 6 grid and make the templates.

"A" Star Variation

A simple but very effective variation on a traditional nine-patch block, this "A" Star Variation forms interesting secondary patterns when repeated. You could make it as a striking scrap quilt, as long as you maintain good contrast between light and dark fabrics in each block.

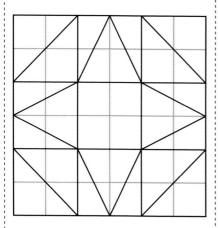

Drafting

Draft the block on a 6 × 6 grid and make the templates.

Cutting guide

Cut out all the fabric in the required shapes as directed.

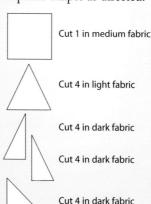

Cut 1 in medium fabric

Cut 4 in light fabric

Cut 4 in dark fabric

Cut 4 in dark fabric

Cut 4 in dark fabric
Cut 4 in light fabric

Chevron Log Cabin

In this easy variation on the basic Log Cabin block (see pages 68 and 146), alternating strips of light and dark fabrics create a chevron effect that, in turn, produces some interesting variations when several blocks are arranged in a quilt. It is not necessary to make templates; just cut strips of the required width, then cut each one to the right length when it has been sewn around the corner square.

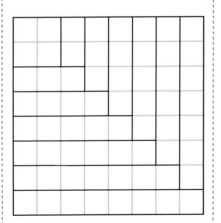

Drafting

Draft the block on an 8 × 8 grid. Measure the square and strip width, and add seam allowances.

Cutting guide

Cut out the corner square and long strips of fabric (these will be cut to length as you work around the block). Keep cutting batches of fabric as you need it if you are making several blocks.

Cut 1 in dark fabric

Cut 3 in light fabric
Cut 3 in dark fabric

Courthouse Steps

In this variation on the basic Log Cabin block (see pages 68 and 146), the dark and light fabrics are placed opposite each other, rather than on two adjacent sides. Although you could make templates and cut the "logs" to the exact sizes required, it is easier to cut long strips of fabric and trim them to the required length after you have sewn them in place.

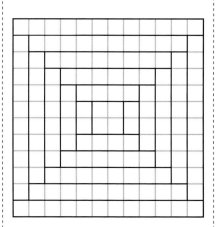

Drafting

Draft the block on a 12 × 12 grid. Measure the square and strip width, and add seam allowances.

Cutting guide

Cut out the center square and long strips of fabric (these will be cut to length as you work around the block). Keep cutting batches of fabric as you need it if you are making several blocks.

☐ Cut 1 in medium fabric

▭ Cut 5 in light fabric
Cut 5 in dark fabric

Drunkard's Path

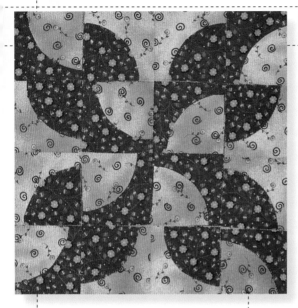

Before 1849 this block was known as Rocky Road to Dublin, but Drunkard's Path is what it is usually called today. It has lots of design potential because the patches can be arranged in many ways. You can piece the curved patches together as described here, or make it really easy by appliquéing the red patches onto squares of fabric and then sewing the squares together.

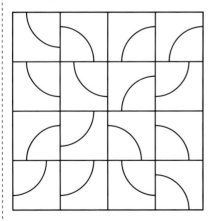

Drafting

Enlarge the block diagram to the required size and make templates.

Cutting guide

Cut out all the fabric in the required shapes as directed.

Cut 8 in dark fabric
Cut 8 in light fabric

Cut 8 in dark fabric
Cut 8 in light fabric

Drunkard's Path quilting patterns

Sewing curved-seam patchwork is just as easy to do by hand as by machine. The seam allowance will naturally fall to one side of the curve and this may dictate how and where you quilt this block. A quilting design that uses curves will accentuate the visual "movement" provided by the curved-seam patchwork.

Contour quilting

Geometric design: directional

Curvilinear design: overlapping circles

Tip There is plenty of scope for quilting with different stitches within this block, which will add further textural interest.

Chevrons

The chevron is a very old pattern, probably derived from the shape made by the meeting of eaves on a roof. As well as featuring frequently on coats of arms and old floor tiles, quilters have exploited the chevron's design value to produce some interesting effects. Other names for this block include Building Blocks, Wave, and Rail Fence.

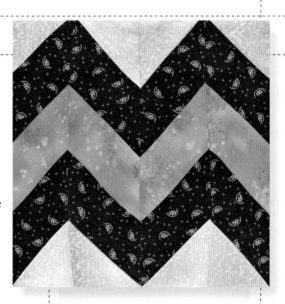

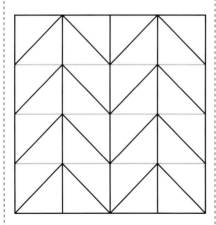

Drafting
Draft the block on a 4 × 4 grid and make the templates.

Cutting guide
Cut out all the fabric in the required shapes as directed.

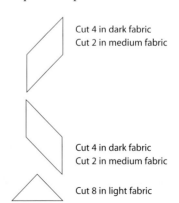

Cut 4 in dark fabric
Cut 2 in medium fabric

Cut 4 in dark fabric
Cut 2 in medium fabric

Cut 8 in light fabric

Left and Right

This intriguing block from the 1930s has a distinctly modern look. It is the sort of pattern seen in Victorian floor tiles, and the colors used here are typical of those that would have been used for that purpose. When repeated blocks are set together, an interesting three-dimensional pattern of boxed tiles appears. The trick is to use dark and light tones of the same color for the bands.

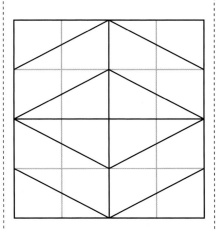

Drafting

Draft the block on a 4 × 4 grid and make the templates.

Cutting guide

Cut out all the fabric in the required shapes as directed.

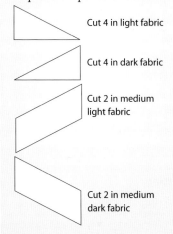

Cut 4 in light fabric

Cut 4 in dark fabric

Cut 2 in medium light fabric

Cut 2 in medium dark fabric

Cross in a Cross

Many blocks dating from the nineteenth century have names that reflect the religious times in which they originated, so there are several blocks featuring crosses. Cross in a Cross is easy to piece if you construct the center square as a separate unit. Repeated blocks set side by side in rows will produce an interesting subsidiary pattern.

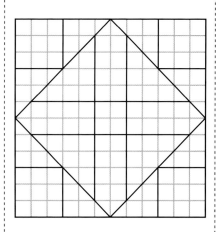

Drafting

Draft the block on a 12 × 12 grid and make the templates.

Cutting guide

Cut out all the fabric in the required shapes as directed.

Cut 4 in light fabric

Cut 8 in dark fabric

Cut 4 in light fabric

Cut 4 in medium fabric

Cut 1 in light fabric

Old Maid's Ramble

Although this seems to have been its most common name, Old Maid's Ramble was also traditionally known as Crimson Rambler and Vermont. The diagonal emphasis of the pattern produces some interesting subsidiary patterns when blocks are repeated.

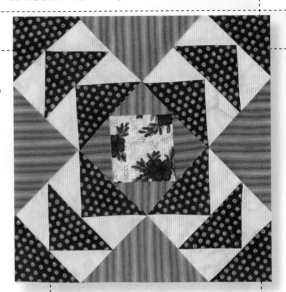

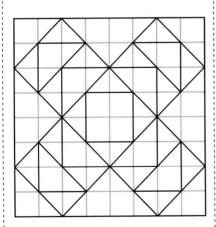

Drafting

Draft the block on an 8 × 8 grid and make the templates.

Cutting guide

Cut out all the fabric in the required shapes as directed.

Cut 1 in medium light fabric

Cut 4 in medium dark fabric
Cut 16 in light fabric

Cut 12 in dark fabric

Cut 4 in medium dark fabric

Jack in the Box

Jack in the Box is also known as Whirligig, which is an apt description of the pattern. Once again, this five-patch pattern has built-in sashings and posts that join up when the blocks are repeated to give the familiar lattice effect.

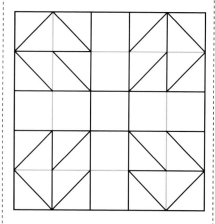

Drafting

Draft the block on a 5 × 5 grid and make the templates.

Cutting guide

Cut out all the fabric in the required shapes as directed.

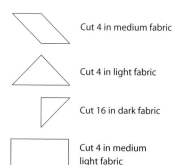

Cut 4 in medium fabric

Cut 4 in light fabric

Cut 16 in dark fabric

Cut 4 in medium light fabric

Cut 1 in dark fabric

Crazy Ann

This interesting block has built-in movement; its other names are Follow the Leader and the descriptive Twist and Turn. Repeated blocks produce the effect of a pieced grid, so when the blocks are joined with sashings, the pattern looks even more complex and the underlying design is seen through layers.

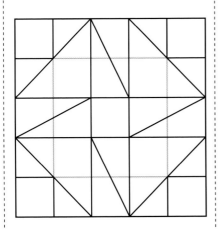

Drafting

Draft the block on a 5 × 5 grid and make the templates.

Cutting guide

Cut out all the fabric in the required shapes as directed.

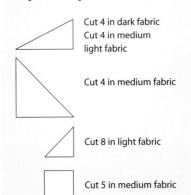

Cut 4 in dark fabric
Cut 4 in medium
light fabric

Cut 4 in medium fabric

Cut 8 in light fabric

Cut 5 in medium fabric

Stonemason's Puzzle

The pattern of this block dates from the 1920s. As with other designs that have built-in sashings, when blocks are repeated the effect is of a completely different pieced block that has been set with sashings and posts. The pattern becomes even more complex if you set the blocks with additional sashings and posts.

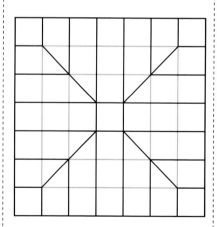

Drafting

Draft the block on a 7 × 7 grid and make the templates.

Cutting guide

Cut out all the fabric in the required shapes as directed.

Cut 4 of light fabric

Cut 4 of medium dark fabric

Cut 4 of light fabric

Cut 4 of medium dark fabric

Cut 5 of dark fabric

Cut 4 of medium light fabric

Seven-patch Flower

This block looks more complicated than it is, with the rectangles appearing to join together as sashings when blocks are repeated. With only thee templates, this is not a difficult block to piece.

Cutting guide

Cut out all the fabric in the required shapes as directed.

Cut 8 of light fabric
Cut 9 of medium fabric
Cut 8 of medium dark fabric

Cut 4 of medium light fabric
Cut 4 of medium dark fabric

Cut 4 of medium light fabric
Cut 4 of medium dark fabric

Cut 4 of dark fabric

Drafting

Draft the block on a 7 × 7 grid and make the templates.

Locked Star

When repeated blocks are joined side by side, the effect is of pieced stars set between plain squares. However, you can vary this effect by using fabrics in different colors on opposite sides of the center square. You could also use a feature fabric for the central square.

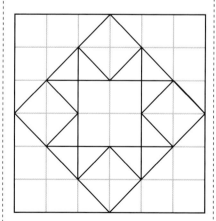

Drafting

Draft the block on a 6 × 6 grid and make the templates.

Cutting guide

Cut out all the fabric in the required shapes as directed.

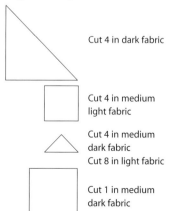

Cut 4 in dark fabric

Cut 4 in medium light fabric

Cut 4 in medium dark fabric
Cut 8 in light fabric

Cut 1 in medium dark fabric

Arrows

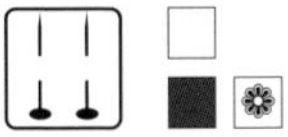

Because this block has only diagonal symmetry, it lends itself to some interesting variations and settings. Only three templates and three fabrics are needed, so this is not a difficult block to make. This example uses a feature fabric for two of the large square patches, but you could replace this with any medium-colored fabric if you prefer.

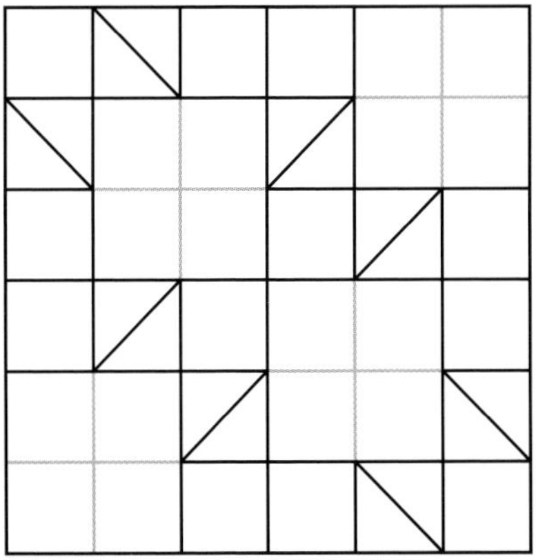

Drafting

Draft the block on a 6 × 6 grid and make the templates.

Cutting guide

Cut out all the fabric in the required shapes as directed.

Cut 2 in light fabric
Cut 2 in feature fabric

Cut 8 in light fabric
Cut 8 in dark fabric

Cut 6 in light fabric
Cut 6 in dark fabric

Basket of Scraps

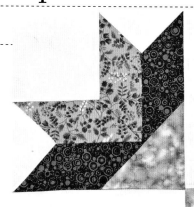

This simple nine-patch block can produce some stunning quilts. As the name suggests, the block really invites you to make it from scraps, but it also works well if you use the same fabrics in every block. The only difficult thing is that patches must be set into the petal shapes, but you could use the English patchwork method to avoid this if you prefer (see page 92).

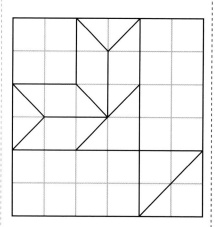

Drafting

Draft the block on a 6 × 6 grid and make the templates.

Cutting guide

Cut out all the fabric in the required shapes as directed.

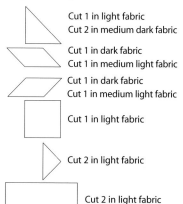

Cut 1 in light fabric
Cut 2 in medium dark fabric

Cut 1 in dark fabric
Cut 1 in medium light fabric

Cut 1 in dark fabric
Cut 1 in medium light fabric

Cut 1 in light fabric

Cut 2 in light fabric

Cut 2 in light fabric

Compass Kaleidoscope

Compass Kaleidoscope is a variation on a traditional Kaleidoscope pattern, with repeated blocks forming an interesting design of circles over the quilt surface. This is a lovely pattern for a scrap quilt, and will still create the effect of circles as long as you maintain the light/dark contrast in each block.

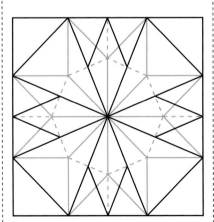

Drafting

Draft the block on an 8-pointed star grid and make the templates.

Cutting guide

Cut out all the fabric in the required shapes as directed.

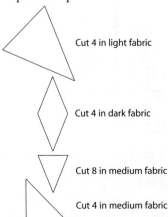

Cut 4 in light fabric

Cut 4 in dark fabric

Cut 8 in medium fabric

Cut 4 in medium fabric

Log Cabin

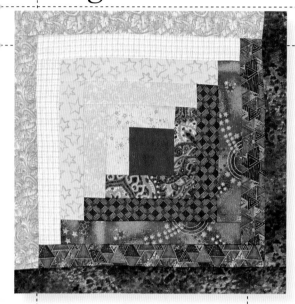

The basic Log Cabin quilt, one of the most popular patchwork patterns ever, can be made from scrap or repeated fabrics. Many different patterns can be produced by changing the arrangement of the blocks in the quilt. You do not need templates for this block and can piece it as described here or use the foundation-piecing technique (see pages 69–70).

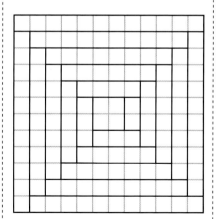

Drafting

Draft the block on a 12 × 12 grid. Measure the square and strip width, and add seam allowances.

Cutting guide

Cut out the center square and long strips of fabric (these will be cut to length as you work around the block). Keep cutting batches of fabric as you need it if you are making several blocks.

Cut 1 in medium fabric

Cut 5 in light fabric
Cut 5 in dark fabric

Log Cabin quilting patterns

Log Cabin patchwork is one of the oldest patterns and has been used extensively, both historically and geographically. This block is constructed using strips of fabric and working in a circular direction emanating outward from the central square.

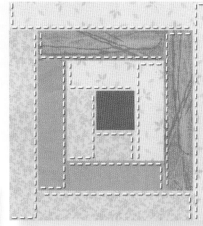

Contour quilting

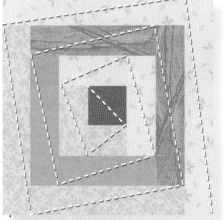

Geometric design: straight line spiral

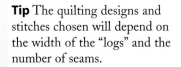

Tip The quilting designs and stitches chosen will depend on the width of the "logs" and the number of seams.

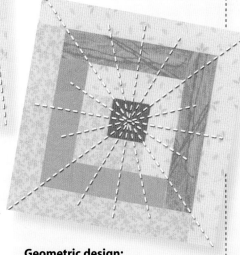

Geometric design: starburst

Off-center Log Cabin

Off-center Log Cabin is a particularly exciting block because repeated blocks create curves even though only straight piecing is used. The pattern is constructed in exactly the same way as a basic Log Cabin block (see pages 68 and 146), but the strips on one side are narrower than those on the other side. You do not need to make any templates.

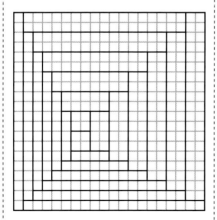

Drafting

Draft the block on a 20 × 20 grid. Measure the square and strip widths, and add seam allowances.

Cutting guide

Cut out the center squares and long strips of fabric (these will be cut to length as you work around the block). Keep cutting batches of fabric as you need it if you are making several blocks.

☐ Cut 1 in light fabric
Cut 1 in dark fabric

▭ Cut 6 in light fabric

▭ Cut 6 in dark fabric

Orange Peel

Although published under this name only since 1898, this is actually a very old pattern also known as Melon Patch and Lafayette. For such a simple idea, it produces some very impressive patterns. It is an easy block to piece because the gentle curves present no problems, but you could make it even easier by appliquéing the petal-shaped patches onto squares of fabric.

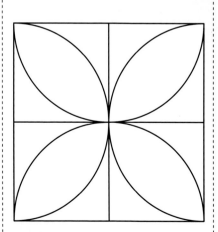

Drafting

Enlarge the block diagram to the required size and make templates.

Cutting guide

Cut out all the fabric in the required shapes as directed.

Cut 2 in dark fabric
Cut 2 in light fabric

Cut 4 in dark fabric
Cut 4 in light fabric

Grandmother's Fan

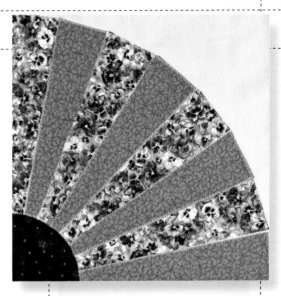

Grandmother's Fan is a very old pattern that probably has its origins in a time when no well-dressed lady's outfit was complete without a fan. It can be made with any number of scrap fabrics and will always look effective. You can piece the whole block from patches, or appliqué the fan—either pieced together first or patch by patch—onto a background square.

Drafting

Enlarge the block diagram to the required size and make templates.

Cutting guide

Cut out all the fabric in the required shapes as directed.

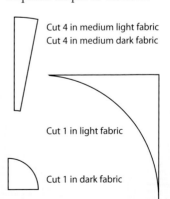

Cut 4 in medium light fabric
Cut 4 in medium dark fabric

Cut 1 in light fabric

Cut 1 in dark fabric

Robbing Peter to Pay Paul

This block gains its effect from the contrasting colors used in the positive/negative placement of the shapes. It works well if you use strong light/dark contrast between the two fabrics. As with many blocks involving curved shapes, you can construct it either by piecing or by appliquéing the outer patches onto squares of fabric.

Drafting

Enlarge the block diagram to the required size and make templates.

Cutting guide

Cut out all the fabric in the required shapes as directed.

Cut 2 in light fabric
Cut 2 in dark fabric

Cut 8 in light fabric
Cut 8 in dark fabric

Mill Wheel

This traditional pattern is also known as Steeplechase, perhaps because it resembles the designs on jockeys' caps. The block is developed from two simple units and makes a delightful scrap quilt if enough contrast is maintained between the fabrics. As with many blocks with curves, you can piece curved patches together as described here or appliqué the circular patches onto squares of fabric.

Cutting guide

Cut out all the fabric in the required shapes as directed.

Cut 8 in dark fabric
Cut 8 in light fabric

Cut 8 in dark fabric
Cut 8 in light fabric

Drafting

Enlarge the block diagram to the required size and make templates.

Japanese Fan

An eye-catching variation on the fan theme, the Japanese Fan dates from the 1930s when there was a vogue for all things Japanese. This is another block that can either be pieced completely or by appliquéing the pieced fan onto a square of background fabric.

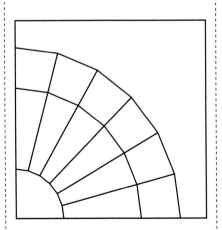

Drafting

Enlarge the block diagram to the required size and make templates.

Cutting guide

Cut out all the fabric in the required shapes as directed.

Cut 3 in dark fabric
Cut 3 in medium light fabric

Cut 3 in dark fabric
Cut 3 in medium light fabric

Cut 1 in medium dark fabric

Cut 1 in light fabric

Rose of Sharon

Wreaths make beautiful appliqué blocks, and some are very complex. This is one of the easier designs, but the circular stem onto which the flowers and petals are appliquéd needs care. Use a compass to draw a double circle on the background square so that you get an accurate shape without the need for a template.

Drafting

Enlarge the block diagram to the required size and make templates.

Cutting guide

Cut out a background square of medium fabric at the size of the finished block, plus a seam allowance. Cut medium light and light fabric in the required shapes as directed, reserving some dark fabric for the stems.

Cut 4 in light fabric

Cut 20 in medium light fabric

Rose of Sharon quilting patterns

There are numerous "wreath" patterns to be found among appliqué designs. Variations can be made in the number and style of flowers and leaves, and whether or not a circular "vine" is included. The style of the wreath can be highlighted effectively by contour quilting.

Contour quilting

Geometric design: diagonal infill lines

Curvilinear design: echo quilting

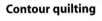

Tip Use an infill pattern to quilt the background fabric and add emphasis to the appliqué.

Mexican Rose

There are several appliqué patterns called Mexican Rose, with this one dating from around 1842. It is unusual in combining geometric shapes with the organic shapes of the petals. Although the same template is used to make all the petals, slight variations would emphasize the organic design without diminishing the overall effect of the pattern.

Drafting

Enlarge the block diagram to the required size and make templates.

Cutting guide

Cut out a background square of medium light fabric at the size of the finished block, plus a seam allowance. Cut dark, medium dark, and light fabrics in the required shapes as directed reserving some medium fabric for the stems.

Cut 4 in dark fabric

Cut 12 in dark fabric
Cut 12 in medium dark fabric

Cut 4 in light fabric

Cut 1 in medium dark fabric

Crossed Canoes

It is important to make accurate templates and take extra care when piecing this block to achieve sharp corner points. To make life really easy, you could piece together four squares and appliqué large triangular patches on top, but you will need to use all three templates if you wish to vary the colors of the small inner triangles.

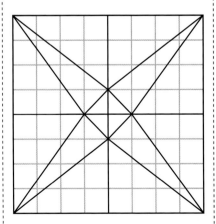

Drafting

Draft the block on an 8 × 8 grid and make the templates.

Cutting guide

Cut out all the fabric in the required shapes as directed.

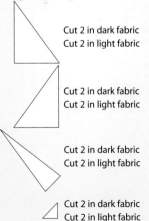

Cut 2 in dark fabric
Cut 2 in light fabric

Cut 2 in dark fabric
Cut 2 in light fabric

Cut 2 in dark fabric
Cut 2 in light fabric

Cut 2 in dark fabric
Cut 2 in light fabric

Wild Rose and Square

When the patches in each corner unit are pieced in different tones of the same color (pink in this example), they produce a three-dimensional effect that is emphasized if dark squares are set into the corners. Apart from the need to set in the seams for the corner squares, the block is straightforward to piece.

Drafting

Draft the block on a 5 × 5 grid and make the templates.

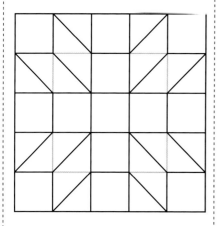

Cutting guide

Cut out all the fabric in the required shapes as directed.

Cut 1 in medium fabric
Cut 4 in medium dark fabric
Cut 4 in light fabric
Cut 4 in dark fabric

Cut 4 in medium fabric

Cut 4 in medium light fabric

Cut 8 in medium dark fabric

Buffalo Ridge

This interesting block appears to be fairly modern. It was first published under this name in 1972, then again as Country Roads in 1979. Repeated blocks produce the effect of an intricately pieced diagonal lattice lying beneath a grid.

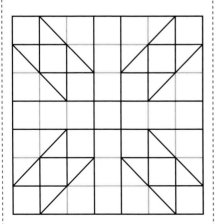

Drafting

Draft the block on a 7 × 7 grid and make the templates.

Cutting guide

Cut out all the fabric in the required shapes as directed.

Cut 13 in medium dark fabric

Cut 4 in medium light fabric

Cut 16 in light fabric

Cut 8 in dark fabric

Greek Cross

This block looks deceptively complex but is easily achieved if you join the seams accurately. Repeated blocks reveal crosses and squares lying beneath a grid, while the light patches around the edges join to form squares and long hexagons.

Drafting

Draft the block on a 7 × 7 grid and make the templates.

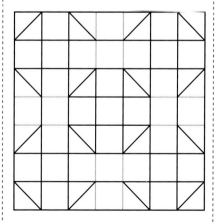

Cutting guide

Cut out all the fabric in the required shapes as directed.

Cut 4 in light fabric

Cut 8 in medium dark fabric
Cut 4 in medium light fabric
Cut 5 in dark fabric

Cut 4 in medium dark fabric

Cut 8 in light fabric
Cut 16 in medium light fabric

Puss in the Corner

This is another block with several aliases, also appearing as Aunt Sukey's Choice and Puss in Boots. Some interesting variations are possible, such as using a different color for the four corner patches.

Cutting guide

Cut out all the fabric in the required shapes as directed.

Cut 8 in light fabric
Cut 9 in medium fabric

Cut 8 in light fabric
Cut 4 in medium fabric
Cut 16 in dark fabric

Cut 4 in light fabric

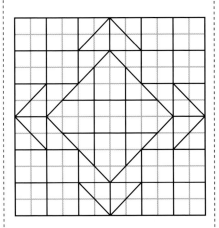

Drafting

Draft the block on a 12 × 12 grid and make the templates.

Shaded Trail

The four center blades should be pieced in two shades of the same color, so that they appear to be faceted. The third fabric forming the background can be either very light or very dark, depending on the tones you have chosen for the other two fabrics. It is easier to stitch this block by hand using the English patchwork method (see page 92).

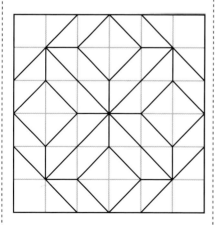

Drafting

Draft the block on a 6 × 6 grid and make the templates.

Cutting guide

Cut out all the fabric in the required shapes as directed. Cut out the same quantities of paper patches, but without a seam allowance.

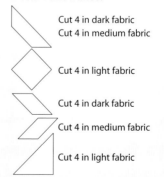

Cut 4 in dark fabric
Cut 4 in medium fabric

Cut 4 in light fabric

Cut 4 in dark fabric

Cut 4 in medium fabric

Cut 4 in light fabric

Illinois

If you are making lots of Illinois blocks, you could sew the side units using the chain piecing method (see page 96) and then use any leftover units to make a pieced border. Alternatively, save them for another quilting project.

Drafting

Draft the block on a 6 × 6 grid and make the templates.

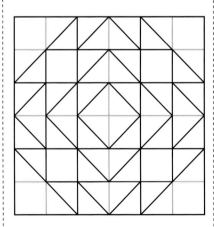

Cutting guide

Cut out all the fabric in the required shapes as directed.

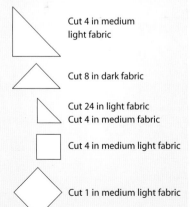

Cut 4 in medium light fabric

Cut 8 in dark fabric

Cut 24 in light fabric
Cut 4 in medium fabric

Cut 4 in medium light fabric

Cut 1 in medium light fabric

Garden Maze

Garden Maze is an intriguing block that, when repeated, produces a complex interlaced pattern that forces the viewer to look closely to see where blocks begin and end. It requires careful piecing to get the pattern right, but this is a good block to choose if you want to create a big impression. Make sure you choose fabrics with good dark/light contrast.

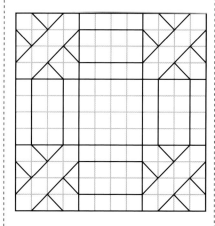

Drafting

Draft the block on a 12 × 12 grid and make the templates.

Cutting guide

Cut out all the fabric in the required shapes as directed.

Cut 1 in medium dark fabric

Cut 4 in light fabric

Cut 4 in medium light fabric
Cut 4 in dark fabric

Cut 2 in medium light fabric
Cut 2 in dark fabric

Cut 4 in medium light fabric
Cut 4 in dark fabric

Cut 16 in light fabric

Star Diamond

This nine-patch star is one of the more complex blocks that are often known as feathered stars. Although it looks complicated, the piecing is broken down into manageable units. Take great care when piecing the corner and side units, however, because the small triangular and square patches are very similar in size and are cut in the same fabrics.

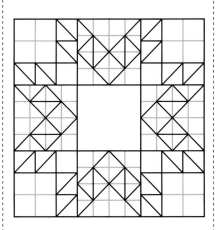

Drafting

Draft a 3 × 3 grid, then divide the corner units into 3 × 3 and the side units into 4 × 4. Make templates.

Cutting guide

Cut out all the fabric in the required shapes as directed.

Cut 1 in feature fabric

Cut 8 in dark fabric

Cut 4 in light fabric

Cut 8 in light fabric
Cut 16 in medium fabric

Cut 4 in light fabric

Cut 16 in light fabric
Cut 16 in medium fabric

Cut 4 in light fabric

Cut 4 in light fabric

Star of the East

Star of the East is a delightful eight-pointed star in which the faceted rays cause it to stand out from its background in a striking way. An alternative to setting in the patches around the star is to appliqué the star onto a square of background fabric.

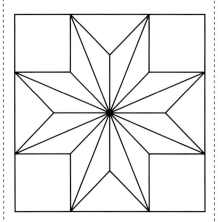

Cutting guide

Cut out all the fabric in the required shapes as directed.

Cut 8 in medium fabric
Cut 8 in light fabric

Cut 4 in dark fabric

Cut 4 in dark fabric

Drafting

Draft the block on an 8-pointed star grid and make the templates.

Star of the East quilting patterns

Many patchwork blocks, such as this one, are not designed on a formal grid. The star can be kept fairly simple, or added to with extra points, along with intricate piecing of the central circle. A simple quilting design is all that is necessary for this patchwork block.

Contour quilting

Geometric design: starburst

Curvilinear design: circles

Tip Use busy quilting stitches in moderation so they do not detract from the pattern itself.

Arkansas Traveler

Arkansas Traveler, also known as Cowboy's Star, was the name of a popular song of the 1860s that was whistled and sung everywhere. The piecing is a little tricky and needs care, but repeated blocks make such lovely patterns that it is well worth the effort.

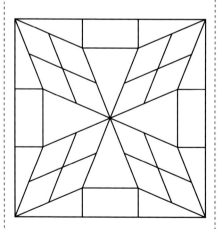

Drafting

Enlarge the block diagram to the required size and make templates.

Cutting guide

Cut out all the fabric in the required shapes as directed.

Cut 8 in light fabric
Cut 8 in dark fabric

Cut 4 in medium light fabric

Cut 4 in medium dark fabric

Cut 4 in medium light fabric

Cut 4 in medium light fabric

Star Upon Stars

Pieced stars are an old favorite, and this one has appeared under several names, including Virginia Star and Unknown Star. When piecing the eight diamonds that form the star, it is useful to have a template of the completed diamond with which to check the accuracy of each one as you finish piecing it.

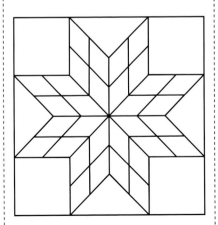

Drafting
Draft the block on an 8-pointed star grid. Divide the blades of the star diagonally in half. Make templates.

Cutting guide
Cut out all the fabric in the required shapes as directed.

Cut 16 in light fabric
Cut 16 in medium fabric

Cut 4 in dark fabric

Cut 4 in dark fabric

Bleeding Hearts

This block looks more complex than it actually is. It is constructed from two different pieced units and a center square; provided you cut the patches with accurate seam allowances, the piecing should not present any problems.

Drafting

Enlarge the block diagram to the required size and make templates.

Cutting guide

Cut out all the fabric in the required shapes as directed.

Cut 1 in medium fabric

Cut 4 in light fabric

Cut 4 in dark fabric

Cut 4 in dark fabric

Cut 4 in dark fabric

Cut 8 in light fabric

Cut 4 in light fabric

Circular Saw

This is an old-time pattern, the name of which, like so many traditional patterns, reflects the surroundings of the women who made them—no doubt saws were important pieces of equipment in pioneer times. The pattern is also known as Oriole Window and Four Little Fans.

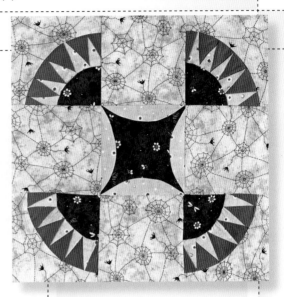

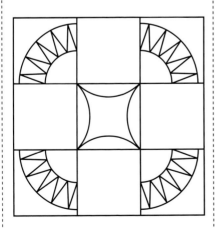

Drafting

Enlarge the block diagram to the required size and make templates.

Cutting guide

Cut out all the fabric in the required shapes as directed.

Cut 1 in dark fabric

Cut 4 in light fabric

Cut 20 in light fabric

Cut 16 in medium dark fabric

Cut 4 in medium dark fabric

Cut 4 in medium dark fabric

Cut 4 in dark fabric

 Cut 4 in medium light fabric

Cut 4 in medium light fabric

Broken Stone

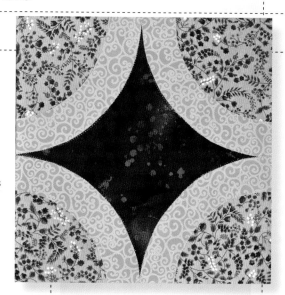

This block from the 1930s has a distinctly period look about it. The curved bands, meeting in repeated blocks to form circles over the quilt surface, need careful piecing so that they meet as accurately as possible, so this is one block you might find easier to sew by hand. You could also simplify it by appliquéing the circular patches onto a large square of fabric.

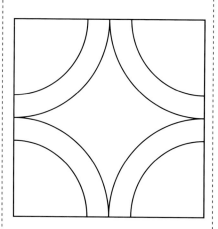

Drafting

Enlarge the block diagram to the required size and make templates.

Cutting guide

Cut out all the fabric in the required shapes as directed.

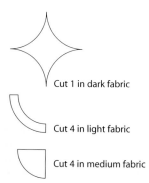

Cut 1 in dark fabric

Cut 4 in light fabric

Cut 4 in medium fabric

Double Wedding Ring

This classic pattern, ever popular for wedding quilts, can produce some striking effects when the colors are varied. It is also often made as a scrap quilt because the strong graphic impact will emerge regardless of how many fabrics are used.

Cutting guide

Cut out all the fabric in the required shapes as directed.

Cut 24 in medium light fabric
Cut 16 in dark fabric

Cut 4 in medium dark fabric
Cut 4 in medium fabric

Cut 4 in light fabric

Cut 8 in light fabric

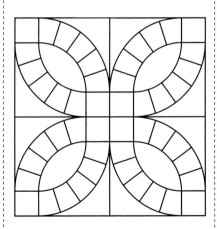

Drafting

Enlarge the block diagram to the required size and make templates.

Snake Trail

The evocatively named Snake Trail has also been published as Rattlesnake and Rocky Road Around California. The block is made from two fans placed in opposite corners of a square, so you can make it by piecing just the fan components and appliquéing them onto a background square or by piecing the whole block.

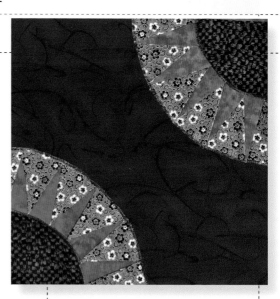

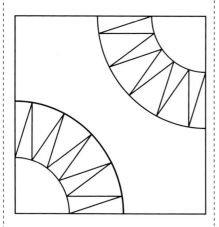

Drafting

Enlarge the block diagram to the required size and make templates.

Cutting guide

Cut out all the fabric in the required shapes as directed.

Cut 8 in light fabric

Cut 10 in medium fabric

Cut 2 in light fabric

Cut 2 in light fabric

Cut 2 in dark fabric

Cut 1 in medium dark fabric

Triple Flower

This appliqué block is a typical folk art design. The diagonal slant of the pattern means that repeated blocks produce some interesting effects. Although each flower head is formed from a single patch, you can embellish the flowers in any way you like when the block is finished. You could also adjust the shapes of the leaves into more organic curves if you prefer.

Drafting

Enlarge the block diagram to the required size and make templates.

Cutting guide

Cut out a background square of light fabric at the size of the finished block, plus a seam allowance. Cut the remaining fabric as directed, reserving some dark fabric for the stems.

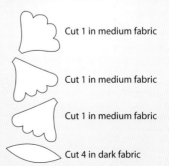

Cut 1 in medium fabric

Cut 1 in medium fabric

Cut 1 in medium fabric

Cut 4 in dark fabric

Shippo (Seven Treasures)

The name is probably a pun on "shi ho" (four directions).

Stitching the sashiko

Cut out a 9½ in. (24 cm) square of fabric and mark a ¼ in. (6 mm) seam allowance all around it. Mark a 1½ in. (4 cm) base grid onto the central square. Use a 3-in. (7.5-cm) diameter circle template to mark the sashiko design. Following the red arrows on the diagram, stitch diagonal wavy lines. Stitch around the pattern in continuous lines. Refer to pages 112–113 for tips on sashiko stitching.

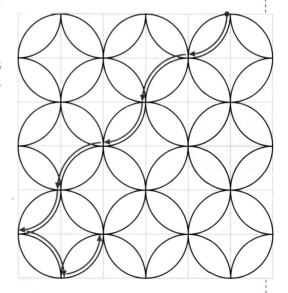

Fundo (Balance Weights)

Gold ingots were traditionally cast in this symmetrical shape.

Stitching the sashiko

Cut out a 9¹/₂ in. (24 cm) square of fabric and mark a ¹/₄ in. (6 mm) seam allowance all around it. Mark a 1¹/₂ in. (4 cm) base grid onto the central square. Use a 3-in. (7.5-cm) diameter circle template to mark the sashiko design. Following the red and blue arrows on the diagram, stitch diagonal wavy lines. Stitch around the pattern in continuous lines. Refer to pages 112–113 for tips on sashiko stitching.

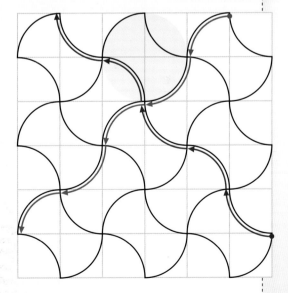

Raimon (Spiral)

This is one of the oldest sashiko designs.

Stitching the sashiko

Cut out a 9½ in. (24 cm) square of fabric and mark a ¼ in. (6 mm) seam allowance all around it. Mark a 4½ in. (12 cm) base grid onto the central square, then mark spirals onto each of the four sections with lines at ½ in. (1 cm) intervals. Note that the diagram below shows only one spiral. Stitch vertical and horizontal lines through the center of the grid. Following the red arrow on the diagram, stitch each spiral. Refer to pages 112–113 for tips on sashiko stitching.

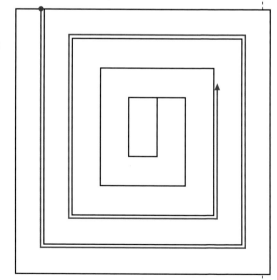

Kagome (Bamboo Basket)

This easy pattern resembles basketweave.

Stitching the sashiko

Cut out a 9¹/₂ in. (24 cm) square of fabric and mark a ¹/₄ in. (6 mm) seam allowance all around it. Mark a ³/₄ × 1¹/₂ in. (2 × 4 cm) base grid onto the central square, then mark the sashiko design. Following the red arrow on the diagram, stitch the vertical lines. Follow the blue and green arrows to stitch diagonal lines. Refer to pages 112–113 for tips on sashiko stitching.

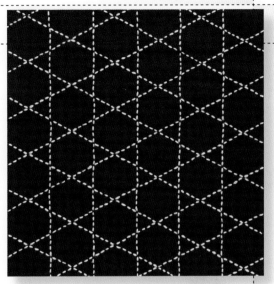

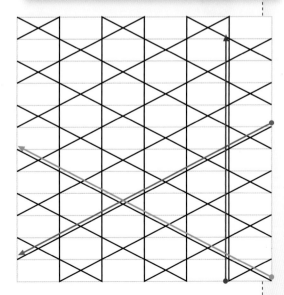

Colonial Knot

The colonial knot is also known as a candlewicking knot. It is very similar in appearance to the French knot, but is slightly larger and sits higher.

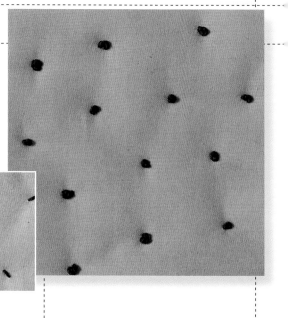

Reverse of work

1 Bring the thread to the surface of the work. Hold the thread over the needle to the right and under the needle to the left; and back over the needle point to the right and under the needle point to the left, as shown.

2 Pull the thread taut to stabilize the knot while you take the needle into the fabric through all layers, just to one side of where the thread initially came out.

3 If you are working several knots within a short distance of each other, make a small quilting stitch on the back, then take the point of the needle into the batting and through to the area for the next knot.

Tip These knots are commonly stitched close together to form a continuous line, but also make a versatile alternative knot for a hand-quilting filling stitch.

Tied Cross

This makes an interesting filling stitch when used on a quilt project. It is possible to vary the size of the cross-stitch legs, but the stitches should remain even.

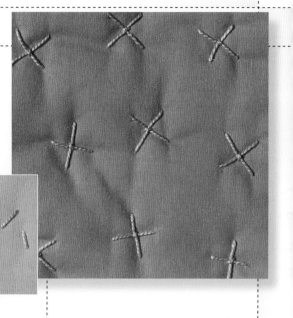

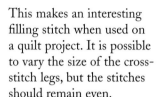

Reverse of work

1 Take the needle into the fabric a short distance away. Make a quilting stitch through all the layers, vertically and upward, bringing the needle out level with where the thread first emerged.

2 Carry the thread across the stitch just produced. Take the needle into the fabric level with the upper leg of the stitch, working diagonally toward the center of the cross, bringing the needle up to one side of it.

3 Take the needle down on the opposite side of the cross, close to the existing threads, to secure it.

4 If working several scattered stitches within a short distance of each other, use this last stitch to quilt through the layers. Make a small quilting stitch on the back, then take the point of the needle into the batting and through to the area for the next stitch.

Resources

In this section you will find all the helpful supporting information, such as a glossary, fabric and equipment stockists, and symbol definitions.

Glossary

American patchwork
Seamed patchwork sewn with hand running stitch or by machine.

Appliqué
Individual shapes sewn to a background fabric.

Backing
The bottom layer of the quilt, under the top and batting.

Backing fabric
Any fabric used for the back of the quilt.

Bagging out
Turning an item right side out after it has been sewn with right sides together, e.g. a cushion. Also used for invisible-edge finish.

Balance marks
Points marked on adjacent patches to be matched when stitching curves. Also known as "notches."

Basting
Large running stitches used to hold two or more layers in position before final sewing or quilting.

Batik
Wax-resist dyed fabrics, often hand dyed.

Batting
The layer placed between the quilt top and the backing, for warmth and appearance.

Bed quilt
A large quilt made to cover the top (and sometimes sides) of a bed, to be viewed laying flat.

Bias strip appliqué
Used to make narrow designs such as flower stems.

Big stitch
Hand quilting with larger running stitches and thicker threads.

Binding
A method of finishing raw edges around the sides of the quilt by enclosing them in strips of folded fabric.

Block
Unit of patchwork made from several pieces. May be repeated or used alone.

Blocking
Easing the finished quilt to lie square and flat, usually by dampening and drying the quilt.

Broderie persé
Printed motifs cut out from fabric and used as appliqué pieces.

Butting
A method of finishing edges by turning them in toward each other.

Chain piecing
Machine sewing patchwork pieces together without cutting the thread between sewn pieces.

Cheater panel
Fabric printed with a large, ready-to-use design, sometimes faux patchwork.

Compass
Mathematical instrument for drawing curves and circles.

Contour quilting
Quilting lines parallel to patchwork seams.

Corded quilting
Designs made by threading cord or thick yarn between parallel lines of stitching.

Counterchange
Reversing colors on a pattern to emphasize negative and positive shapes.

Coverlet
Patchwork bedcover with backing but no batting.

Crazy patchwork
Patchwork made from randomly shaped pieces, usually appliquéd. May include lace, ribbon, embellishments, etc.

Cross hatching
Quilting in a grid pattern, regular or variable.

Darning foot
A sewing machine foot used when the machine feed is disengaged for free-motion quilting.

Directional print
Fabric with motifs in one direction, sometimes in stripes, with an obvious right way up.

Echo quilting
Quilting a series of parallel lines following the outline of a shape, often used for appliqué.

Embellishment
Anything that can be sewn decoratively to the quilt front.